WALKING THE CORPORATE BEAT

Police School for Business People

MICHAEL TABMAN

ISBN: 1-4392-5560-1
ISBN-13: 9781439255605

Visit www.booksurge.com to order additional copies.

DEDICATED TO

My wife, Barbara, who was always at my side.
My friend and partner Christine, who always pushed me.
And my dad, who now watches over me…we miss you.

TABLE OF CONTENTS

WALKING THE CORPORATE BEAT

Police School for Business People

INTRODUCTION

"All units, ten-three, hold all radio traffic for emergency broadcast."

We stopped and waited.

"Scout Thirty-six Adam," the dispatcher called.

"Scout Thirty-six Adam," my partner repeated into the radio, acknowledging the dispatcher.

"Scout Thirty-six Adam, a gang fight in progress, chains and knives, no complainant, respond to location."

Wow, I thought for a second; that sounded like an exciting call. Adrenaline pumping, heart racing, I just about jumped out of my car seat. A gang fight, now that's the kind of call a young, rookie police officer hoped for. My training partner for that night had a much different reaction than mine. He slowly put down his cup of coffee, finished writing his report from the last domestic dispute call we handled, and then casually headed out to this supposedly urgent call. No lights, no sirens. He was not in a rush. Why?

All cops were running with their nightsticks in hand to the scene of a riot. I was told to stop. Why?

"Scout Three-eighty-one Adam, subject is armed with a small handgun." I didn't search him. Why?

I issued the pretty girl a traffic ticket but still got a date. Why?

I found the bank robbery getaway car but was scolded over the FBI radio. Why?

I found an FBI fugitive but was scolded over the radio again. Why?

Two criminals were caught near the scene of a crime. They could have easily gotten away with one year in jail but probably wound up with ten. Why?

If you have one cow and one pig, you really have three animals. Why?

The answers to these questions are not clear, at least not on the surface. How they are all related to one another is probably even less clear. You probably have already tried to answer some of the questions or guess what happened. You may have already passed judgment as to whether someone was right or wrong. Yet, in some instances, there is no right or wrong. The reasons people do or do not do things are the product of many factors: nature, nurture, environment, values and beliefs, life experiences, gut feelings, and individual perceptions.

To answer these questions is to delve into more than just the intricacies of police work, as evidenced by the question of the cow and the pig. There are a handful of concepts and personal attributes that I have observed in my twenty-seven years of law enforcement that I believe are integral to handling stressful and difficult situations successfully. Those concepts and attributes can also be key ingredients to success in business. This is not the same as looking at personality traits or habits common to successful CEOs or management concepts for effective leadership or increasing sales. These questions explore some interesting aspects of human nature; group dynamics; instinct; integrity; ego and judgment, and how they all intertwine. The answers to these questions will even look at how certain, and rather mundane principles of accounting can find their way into the police world. More surprisingly, these concepts go beyond the police world and may address some of the many issues you face in your daily work life. We will see how as we answer these questions and look at many other police situations that offer insight into some of life's little lessons for the average businessperson.

CHAPTER 1

Lesson: <u>Stop and Think</u>
Or, "Ten-four, dispatch. Standing by and waiting for backup."

I became a rookie police officer in 1980 in Fairfax County, Virginia, shortly after graduating from college. At the time, the Fairfax County Police Department was a modern, progressive police department of approximately six hundred officers serving a community with a population somewhere near seven hundred thousand. Fairfax was a bedroom community of Washington D.C. with a moderate crime problem. Murders were rare; I think I responded to two in my three years of service there. Rapes and robberies were more prevalent, probably consistent with communities of that size. Overall, it was a nice place to live and work.

The police department operated on the concept of high visibility—as you drove around Fairfax County, you would see many patrol cars cruising the streets. Think of this from an advertising perspective. When advertising, the intent of high visibility is to keep a certain product in the public's mind. The intent of high visibility from a police perspective is not dissimilar—it is to keep the police on the public's and potential criminals' minds, hopefully deterring crime. Of course, deterrence cannot be measured. There is no realistic way of knowing if somebody chose not to commit a crime for fear of being caught. So how do you measure the efficacy of high visibility? When the crime problem appears to be under relative control, based on comparative statistical studies with similar-sized communities, you can reasonably claim success. That is not much different than comparing your sales and revenue to those of your rival competitor.

Fairfax County was also a service-oriented police department, answering almost all calls for service from the community, even if not really police related, and usually with a quick response time.

Having served on patrol for two years, before being promoted to the Tactical Team, I proved to be one of those cops who had more traffic tickets on the court dockets than most of the other officers. Now, all these years later, I have a much different view of traffic enforcement and I would probably not issue half of those tickets. What seemed important to a twenty-three-year-old rookie cop does not seem quite as important now, from the perspective of being retired after a life spent in law enforcement. And yes, I have gotten a speeding ticket and did not like it. Thankfully, as we grow, our perspective becomes more mature and, thus, more valuable to society. Unfortunately, we are not always in a position to serve society with our newfound maturity.

The Fairfax County Police Department used single-man patrol cars. My designation was Scout 381 Adam. Scout meant a patrol unit. My sector was 38. The 1 indicated that I was the second patrol unit in sector 38; it was a big, busy sector. Adam signified the patrol squad. There were five squads: Adam, Bravo, Charlie, Delta, Echo. My partner with whom I shared the sector was Carl, Scout 38 Adam. We will hear more about him later. Most calls for service did not require a two-man response. When they did, such as calls for domestic disputes or possible crimes in progress, there were usually sufficient officers available and close by to respond quickly. During training, a new officer was partnered up with a field-training officer, usually a senior, well-respected officer who, in police lingo, "knew his shit." For broader experience, the rookie would ride with other senior officers during different shifts. I found the different styles and personalities fascinating in view of the fact they all got the job done effectively and within the law, just in their own way.

Similarly, in business, your employees will have their own styles and own techniques. Some of those work habits may be contrary to your style; you may even find those habits irritating. What is important though is whether they get the work done on time, with the expected results. If so, then accept them for who they are and how they work.

My first training officer was an experienced officer I will call Kevin Roberts. He was bright, with a low-key personality and a subdued sense of humor, and had a reputation as a straight shooter. One night shift, around the second week of my being on the job, Roberts and I were called to the scene of a riot. It was not a real riot, but it was somewhat of a mess. On a major intersection, a large number of bikers and rednecks were getting rowdy and out of control. No major fights or assaults were going on, but the scene was chaotic and very tense with a lot of scuffling, pushing, and shoving that was clearly on the verge of escalating, perhaps into a riot situation. This all started with the forceful arrest of one of the crowd's members. Roberts and I arrived on the scene with a number of other patrol units. Cops came flying out of their cars, batons in hand and fleeing into the fray. I was just about to follow the others, when Roberts put out his arm and stopped me.

"What are you planning to do?" he asked. I thought for a moment and realized that I had no idea what I was about to do. Quite hesitantly, I admitted it.

"So why are you running over there waving that big ole nightstick?" was his next question. Answering, "Because everyone else is," was clearly not the correct answer for a rookie trying to impress his training officer. I just gave my blank stare, acknowledging my ignorance.

Roberts then got on the radio to find a sergeant and asked the sergeant if he was taking command and if there was a plan of action—a polite hint. The sergeant took the hint, assumed command and control, and laid out a sensible plan of action. We regrouped, cordoned off the crowd with minimal force using proper riot control techniques, and resolved the issue with few arrests and injuries. I looked at my partner and knew right away that this police officer was going to rise in the ranks. He took the time to stop and think.

I remember one time when I was riding with another cop on the squad; I'll call him Tommy. Tommy was known to be a good and reliable cop. He always wore short sleeves, which had been tailored to highlight his impressive biceps. Tommy was not a cop you wanted to tangle with. That day we were assigned to serve a mental petition. A mental petition was a court order to take someone into custody involuntarily and bring him to a mental health facility to be confined. These were extremely unpleasant assignments, for obvious reasons. It was nothing a young police officer in training wanted to spend his time on. Since there was no way out of it, I wanted to go out and get it done as quickly as possible, so we could be ready for the next call. As Tommy was reading over the court order, I could see he was giving it some serious thought.

"Hmm, she's fifty-three years old and about a hundred forty pounds. I'll call for backup."

"What!" I exclaimed in disbelief. "You and I can't lock up a fifty-three-year-old woman?"

I was shocked at his suggestion. Somehow, I managed to talk Tommy out of calling for backup. We got to the house and began the process of taking her into custody involuntarily. It took only a few minutes for me to realize that I had a lot to learn. There we were, two young cops, both in very good shape, rolling around on the floor with this old (in our twenty-something view) woman, trying to subdue her and get her handcuffed. It was not easy, and to my surprise, she was putting up quite a fight. Also, keep in mind that we were trying to accomplish this using minimal force. Fortunately, her husband, who broke down into tears, did not snap and grab a kitchen knife or, even worse, go for one of our guns. A wrestling match is never a good tactic for police officers; it is an easy way to have their guns taken from them. Looking back on it now, seeing the two of us wrestling with this woman, I get a good laugh. I learned my lesson. Tommy stopped and thought things out based on his years of experience. His only mistake was listening to me.

Here is just a little bit of information for you to consider. About a year later, I was again assigned the unenviable task of having to serve a mental petition on a young man who was about eighteen years of age. As soon as I arrived at the home, I could tell that he came from a good family and his parents were only doing what they felt was best for him. They were suffering at the thought of a police officer carrying off their son to be committed to a mental health facility. When I went to handcuff him, his father politely asked if I could refrain from handcuffing his son. The father acknowledged that his son was troubled—he was suicidal, but he was not dangerous to others. I really felt for this father and the entire family, who were watching from across the living room. I thought about the father's request for a second, but only a second. Then, I quickly realized that I'd better follow established procedures and do it by the book. I handcuffed him, and the family members broke out into tears. When I brought the young man in to the mental health facility, I spoke to the doctor about the father's request; I wanted to know if not handcuffing him would have been safe. The doctor told me, "Officer, never forget what I am about to tell you. Anyone who is suicidal is potentially homicidal." That was enough for me. I was glad I stopped to think and followed the rules.

While I do not have the expertise to know if that is true, and that was just one doctor's informal opinion, it does make sense. If someone is prepared to take his own life, does he really have concern for your life? You must remain alert to changes in your employees' personalities and behavior; you should be knowledgeable of warning signs that may indicate potential violence or suicidal tendencies.

The faster you must react, then, of course, the less time you have to think about your response. In the FBI, we generally did not have to respond to events as quickly and without warning as did police officers. The FBI usually had the benefit of time, of being able to stop and think. If you use that time, it must be used wisely. You cannot rely on, "That's the way we've always done it," or, "We have never had any problems before."

Relying on those premises was a dangerous approach. However, I saw that often in the FBI, and usually in planning arrests. The FBI was often able to make arrests with time to plan and had access to more manpower and weapons than necessary, so most arrests were executed safely. Because of that, agents developed a false sense of security. I observed that bravado many times in my career; agents needed to be slowed down. Agents often became miffed when I required that their arrest plans contain a diagram of the location, each person's assigned position, and a statement assuring that each member of the arrest team knew the location of each other member of the arrest team and that they could recognize each other by sight. Why was that important?

One well-known FBI arrest that went bad occurred in 1985 when the first female agent of the FBI was killed in the line of duty. Before I make any further mention of this arrest, I must point out that I was not there and have no inside information about what occurred. To be consistent with later lessons, this is not meant to be judgmental; we are just trying to learn a lesson. What is known about this tragedy is that she was shot by fellow agents in a case of mistaken identity, what is called friendly fire. A horrendous error led to her death. We must wonder if, before going on this arrest, these FBI agents took the time to stop and think about all the risks involved in the operation. In this case, the obvious question was whether everybody had a chance to look at and recognize the faces of all the other members of the arrest team and knew where they were positioned. Although I am confident the involved agents generally knew their stuff and were highly trained and competent, I would imagine that there had to have been a failure to stop and think before taking action. I would also guess that the failure to stop and think was based upon that unreliable sense of comfort and assuredness that came from so many previous arrests that went off without a hitch. Past successes cannot be the rationale for failing to stop, think, and plan for contingencies, especially if you have the time.

Another significant matter in FBI history that may have reflected a failure to stop and think occurred during the August 2001 arrest of Zacharias Moussaoui, who was often referred to as the twentieth hijacker of 9/11. As of 2009, Mohammad al-Qahtani was being dubbed the twentieth hijacker and Moussaoui was all but forgotten as he serves a life sentence.

In January 2005, I reported as the Special Agent in Charge, known as SAC, of the Minneapolis FBI Office— the office in which Moussaoui was arrested. I received numerous briefings on the matter, read several key reports, and spoke to people from both the field and headquarters who were involved in the matter. There were many different opinions—and they were just opinions—within the FBI as to what role Moussaoui played in the September 11 attacks, though he eventually pled guilty to conspiracy, was sentenced to death, and as of early 2009, was appealing that sentence.

The news that made headlines after 9/11 was that supervisors at FBI headquarters did not approve a search warrant for Moussaoui's belongings at the time of his arrest, prior to 9/11. There was another side to this story. The warrant that the agents requested was a Foreign Intelligence Surveillance Act, known as a FISA warrant, which was different than a criminal search warrant. A FISA warrant was utilized for intelligence gathering, such as for terrorism or foreign espionage activities, and was obtained with the approval of a FISA Court; it required showing that the individual being targeted was an agent of a foreign power, which was specifically defined. Per the laws at that time in history, Moussaoui did not fall within the definition of an agent of a foreign power. Although the Intelligence Reform and Terrorism Prevention Act of 2004 changed that rule via the "Lone Wolf" Amendment, that was the law in 2001.

The supervisors at headquarters, who handled FISA requests as a regular part of their job, did not believe that the requirements for obtaining a FISA warrant had been met. On the surface, and in view of the 9/11 attacks, that decision was being played as a "blunder." However, there is an indication that the field agents who handled this matter did not stop and think to take a critical review of their own work.

First, as pointed out in the public version of a report of the Department of Justice (DOJ), Office of the Inspector General (OIG) entitled *A Review of the FBI's Handling Intelligence Information Related to the September 11 Attacks, US Department of Justice Office of the Inspector General*, released in June 2006, the investigation was opened within one hour of hearing about Moussaoui via a telephone call from flight instructors where Moussaoui was taking flying lessons. The first question to be answered was why was an intelligence case opened so quickly after the phone call? The DOJ OIG report noted, "…the options in the Moussaoui case needed to be evaluated carefully before making the initial decision whether to proceed criminally or as an intelligence investigation under FISA. This was especially true because the Moussaoui case was unusual for the FBI…Unfortunately, this careful or thorough analysis did not occur."

The next question to be answered was why didn't the agents seek a criminal search warrant after headquarters declined the request for a FISA warrant? That would have been relatively easy. According to the DOJ OIG report, when asked that question, one agent who was intimately involved replied, "I never thought about it." He stated that he "…could have done that but it did not occur to [him]." Another agent with an important role in the case, per the DOJ OIG report, "…did not know why a criminal warrant was not sought once the FISA route was exhausted." From the facts that were known at the time, the probable cause for a criminal search warrant was jumping off the page. Why did the agents in the field not pursue a criminal search warrant? Other than what is stated above, my suspicion, and my opinion only, is that the agents were moving so quickly, focused on being right and proving headquarters wrong, they operated with blinders on and did not see an obvious solution. By not stepping back, stopping, and thinking about the situation from an unemotional perspective, opportunity was lost. There are different opinions as to whether a search of Moussaoui's computer and belongings could have unearthed the September 9/11 plot. We will never know.

Just for full disclosure, in September 2006, I reassigned one of the agents involved in criticizing FBI headquarters' performance in the Moussaoui case to another squad within the office. The DOJ OIG ruled that, by that act, I had engaged in retaliation, despite my documentation of insubordination, previous similar conduct by the agent, and having received concurrence of FBI Legal Counsel. Because of that decision, which surprised me, I got spanked by the FBI.

Maybe I should not have been so surprised by that DOJ decision. We are now hearing about the DOJ's alleged involvement in authorizing torture, and in 2006 there were allegations of United States Attorneys being fired for political reasons. In 2005, the Attorney General directed the FBI to initiate investigations of adult pornography, while the FBI was still struggling with the work force demands of staffing terrorism squads. Retired and looking back at an illogical turn of events, I wonder what the environment at the DOJ was at that time—was anybody really stopping to think about anything?

The faster you move, the narrower your field of vision becomes. That is true both literally and figuratively. Sometimes you just have to stop and think, though you believe you know what to do and are ready to act. In an attempt to appear strong and decisive, many managers, especially in law enforcement, snap to a quick decision. That looks good for the moment but often can lead to poor decision making.

Do you have all the facts, and have you considered all the implications and nuances of your decision?

Law enforcement, probably second to the military, is one field where spontaneous decision-making is required more routinely than in regular business. However, even after twenty-seven years in the police business, I have witnessed far fewer instances where a decision needed to be made immediately than you would imagine. This is meant primarily from a management perspective, not out working the street, where decisions must be made in nanoseconds.

Taking time to think things out is often the responsible and most reliable path to take. Yet, to see someone sitting at a desk and just thinking would probably be viewed as useless daydreaming or mental weakness—an inability to make a decision. If you have the time, use it wisely. As well, there is nothing wrong about changing your mind now and then, but you do not want to be forced to change your decisions frequently or, worse, hold on to a bad decision so as not to appear indecisive or insecure. That is what will happen if you make decisions too quickly. You have gotten to your position because of your abilities, hopefully. Have confidence in yourself and your decisions.

So, what about my training officer Kevin Roberts, the cop who first showed me the value of stopping and thinking? Within a few months after that incident, he was promoted to sergeant. Although I left the police department three years later to join the FBI, I maintained my friendships there. Years later, I heard that Roberts was promoted to a command position just below the chief level. No surprise.

By the time I retired in early 2007, every law enforcement officer in the country should have known to conduct himself as if he were being taped—as he probably was. Yet in 2009, a news station asked me to comment on a video of police officers appearing to beat a suspect after he was arrested and handcuffed. I would never make a definitive conclusion based solely on watching a few minutes of tape, but it certainly did not look good for the officers. Cops know not to allow themselves to lose control—that is a career killer, not to mention criminal and civil liability. Just one moment to stop and think would have probably saved these officers from what will likely be a trial by video. When conducting your personal and business affairs, especially when you are worked up and emotional, do not become one of those cops running into the fray waving a nightstick.

On many occasions, you can take time to stop and think before you make a decision. Just remember, as we have said and as I have experienced, not all good decisions have good results.

For those occasions when you do not have time to stop and think, you must be prepared to…

CHAPTER 2

Lesson: Think on Your Feet
Or, "All units discontinue surveillance and make arrests ASAP."

In the late 1980s and into the early 1990s, cocaine became the drug of choice in America. Cocaine was smuggled in from Colombia in massive amounts that would defy the wildest speculations. During that time, I was working as an FBI agent on a drug task force with New York City Police Department detectives. Our office was in Jackson Heights, Queens, in New York City. Short of Colombia itself, Jackson Heights was probably the epicenter of the cocaine drug trade.

We did not have to look too far to find work, just walk out the door. Many times, the work found us. Often, some disgruntled drug dealer got ripped off or thought he was going to be killed or just wanted to use the FBI to eliminate a competitor. So, he became an informant. Hesitantly, I must admit that the motivation did not really bother us. As long as the information was good, we could deem it "reliable," and more importantly, we did not *know* that he was committing any crimes, we would use him as an informant. The only catch—we just could not *catch* him dealing drugs; then we would have to stop using that informant, as we could not turn a blind eye to criminal activity. Working informants was a dirty business and a slippery slope. Many people did not like the concept of the FBI cooperating with drug dealers, mobsters, and all sorts of other criminals. We needed informants; who else could we use?

In the mid 1990s, I opened an investigation on one drug dealer whom we identified from a separate, ongoing undercover operation. Let's call the drug dealer Oscar. The difficulty with this investigation was that I was not able to use any of the information from the undercover operation to do some of the good stuff we did in drug investigations, such as tapping his phone, planting a microphone, etc. Those procedures required a warrant, and a warrant required probable cause, which was to be spelled out in an affidavit. All my probable cause came from the undercover operation that we were not ready to expose. I had to build what we called a parallel case—in other words, starting from scratch. The only option readily available was surveillance. That is what we did. We assigned a special surveillance group to follow Oscar during the day. For two weeks, they followed him; and what did they see? Not much.

Oscar would drive around the Bronx, a borough of New York City; look at his pager; and then go to a pay phone. Remember, there were not a lot of cell phones around at this time. Oscar would meet people on the street, have brief conversations with them, leave, and then meet the same people somewhere else. No criminal activity was observed. We probably had the wrong person, right?

Wrong.

Oscar did not have a job but owned property; he frequently answered his pager by going to pay phones and meeting the same people in different places. True, there was nothing criminal about that in and of itself. This type of conduct, however, was a classic sign of drug trafficking, at least in the early 1990s.

My supervisor was impatient with the lack of progress (i.e. no drugs seized) and pressured me to pull the plug on the case. If we could not come up with something "actionable" against Oscar soon, he believed that there was better use of the surveillance team. I was anxious. I knew I had the right guy, but I just did not know how I could assure that we would be arresting him shortly. I begged for another two weeks, and reluctantly, my supervisor consented. A week and a half went by, and the surveillance unit kept seeing the same things over and over. Suspicious activities? Yes. Criminal activities? No. And, there was nothing we could do about it.

One day I was driving home at rush hour, in the rain, eastbound on the Long Island Expressway. You must be a New Yorker to truly understand that kind of traffic. While stuck in that traffic, I got a call on the radio from the surveillance squad team leader. They were following Oscar and had just observed some activity they found truly suspicious.

Oscar met someone at a street corner, whom the surveillance team dubbed "Yellow Jacket," because he was wearing a bright yellow jacket. Such bright, noticeable clothing is a real boon for a surveillance team. Oscar and Yellow Jacket then split up. The surveillance team followed Oscar to JFK Airport. There, Oscar met up with Yellow Jacket again. Then they met two more individuals who had just flown in from Puerto Rico. Those two gave Oscar and Yellow Jacket four suitcases. They each took two of the suitcases and put them into their own cars. One of the guys who flew in from Puerto Rico went with Yellow Jacket, and the other immediately flew back to Puerto Rico. Once again, there was nothing illegal about these activities on their own. However, to an agent working on drug investigations for a number of years, it certainly smacked of drug trafficking.

The surveillance team had only enough units to follow one vehicle. What did I want them to do? There really was no one right answer. There were many variables and endless possibilities of what was happening. I had to make a decision, and I had to make it fast. As we discussed earlier, the need for these immediate decisions do not arise as often as we would believe. When they do arise, you have to make them—not only because it is your responsibility, but also because you must be able to display confidence, decisiveness, and competence to your subordinates and coworkers. If you appear indecisive or insecure, someone else will make the decision for you. You will have lost all credibility, and that one weak moment is how you will be remembered. Be strong.

I cannot say that I knew exactly what to do, but I went for my best guesstimate. The objective of this investigation was to make a prosecutable case against Oscar. Given the drug trade, anything was possible. Oscar's suitcases could have just been a distraction; they could have been clothes. If we hit him and came up empty, the investigation was over with nothing to show for it. That simply was not an option. We had a game plan. There was reliable intelligence information that Oscar was trafficking drugs, and nothing changed to make us think he had stopped. We had spent weeks following Oscar; what would be the purpose of changing our plans now? I made my decision: follow Oscar's car and let the other one go.

In desperation, I made a call back to the squad room. Maybe I could get some other agents and detectives to head out to JFK Airport and find the second car, something that had a very small likelihood of success. Surveillance had given us a rather detailed description of the car. Calling the office, I got lucky and found a few agents and detectives who were still hanging around. After hearing what was happening, they scrambled to the airport. There were only a few ways out of the airport, so we set our vehicles up on the sides of those roads and hoped and waited, and hoped a little more.

I was getting close to the airport when I heard an amazing call on the radio. One of the agents actually found that second car as it was leaving the airport, and he was following it. I was only moments behind. The surveillance team was still on Oscar. The next question to answer was, "What do we do now?" There were a number of options available, and I had only a few minutes, not many, but a few, to give things some thought. There comes a time when you must execute your plan. All business courses will teach you that planning is easy; execution is where most failures occur.

After doing a quick risk/reward ratio, literally on the run, I decided to stop the vehicle we were following and let the surveillance team keep following Oscar as he was heading back to the Bronx. After all, Oscar was the main target; why take a risk at that moment if I did not have to? Making two different decisions on the run was high risk, but I had to do it.

We pulled over the car on the Whitestone Expressway in Queens, right before the exit for the Whitestone Bridge, which led to the Bronx. That they were heading to the same place as Oscar was a good sign as it added to our probable cause. We interviewed the two occupants of the car. Their stories simply did not gel. Not surprisingly, they did not give permission to search the suitcases. I decided to search them anyway, believing it was a legal search but knowing their defense attorneys would immediately try to quash the search as unconstitutional. There were two suitcases in the trunk. After breaking open the paper-thin locks with one easy tug, I then opened the suitcases. What did we find? We found sixty kilograms of cocaine. Considering that at the time, a single kilogram of cocaine would sell for approximately $30,000. That equaled, well…a lot of money worth of drugs. That was a nice haul.

In the meantime, Oscar was seen taking his suitcases to an apartment in the Bronx. Now I slowed down and took some time to stop and think; there was no need to take further risks. With the drugs we had just found, I was able to get a search warrant for that apartment where Oscar was. Guess what we found there—another thirty kilos of cocaine with some weapons and explosives. We also learned that Yellow Jacket was a fugitive who was looking at thirty years in prison. Not a bad day.

The next morning, after the excitement of making such a nice bust wore off, my partner and I started bemoaning the reality that seizing ninety kilos of cocaine made a great case but did not really put a dent in the tons and tons of cocaine and other drugs that were flooding our cities. One of the agents came up to us and said, "Hey, that's ninety kilos of cocaine that won't make it into some high school in the Bronx; just be proud that you stopped that." He was right. We did the best job we could, trying to keep drug trafficking and other crimes from overwhelming us and plunging us into chaos. That was the best we could hope for.

A few months later at trial and as expected, the defense attorneys moved to suppress the evidence, arguing that I searched the suitcases without probable cause. That was always the first step in a drug case, to try to suppress the evidence. The prosecuting attorney told me that we would probably lose that motion in court, suggesting that the search may not have been legal. Knowing that the prosecutor was wrong, that this search was completely legal, via what is known as the Carroll Doctrine, and also knowing that telling a prosecutor that he was wrong was asking for trouble, I sat down and wrote out for the prosecutor all the arguments as to why the search was legal. In its simplest terms, the Carroll Doctrine allows for warrantless searches of automobiles when probable cause is present. I will not go into all the details, but ultimately, the judge ruled the searches were legal. The judge stated that with all the activities observed, when viewed through the eyes of an experienced narcotics agent, no conclusion other than drug trafficking could have reasonably been drawn by the agent. Oscar and his buddies are probably all still in jail as of this writing.

During these events, I was not positive that every decision I made was the right one. Had those suitcases not had drugs in them, I would have blown the investigation. Had I not been able to convince the judge I had probable cause to search that first suitcase, Oscar and his friends would have gone free and moved elsewhere to traffic in drugs. I had to think on my feet, relying on my experience, training, and gut. This was no different than any other business decision that has to be made on the fly. Use your best judgment and always act in good faith.

Drug arrests are dangerous business operations; you need to do things the right way. One time, I was leading an arrest team to execute a search warrant on a suspected drug house. We had the warrant and were at the right address. We knocked on the door, announced our presence, and waited for a response, which did not come. Accordingly, we made a dynamic entry forcing the door open and charging in announcing ourselves. Well, we had the right address, but we had bad intelligence. We ran right into a vestibule serving about four different apartments, all with their doors closed. We did not know which apartment was the right apartment. Our presence was well known; we had been quite vocal. Anyone or everyone from those apartments could have come out shooting. Where were we? We were stuck right in the middle, sitting ducks for an ambush. It did not take a lot of experience to realize we were in trouble. We did not have a tactical advantage; we were quite exposed. Against basic instinct, I called for us to retreat—to get out of the building—which is not something we normally do. There was certainly a downside to this course of action. Evidence could have been destroyed. Drug dealers inside may have decided to arm themselves, knowing we were there. Everything in life is a trade-off. Standing in the middle of that vestibule was suicidal.

We regrouped, quickly identified the right apartment, and served the warrant without incident. Again, there was a risk/reward ratio to be analyzed right there and right then. My experience and training told me that just standing there, unsure of what to do, posed a much greater risk than a retreat. Sometimes, you just have to rethink your initial actions and seamlessly move to plan B.

Another example of thinking on your feet comes from what should have been a routine call when I was a patrol officer. That decision had a nice payoff, though not immediately. Carl and I were called to a home where a young man had just ingested a large amount of pills and medication in a suicide attempt. He was not falling asleep; instead, he was reacting violently. Carl and I arrived at the scene simultaneously, when the young man drove off at a high rate of speed. He now posed a danger to himself and the community, and we took off in a high-speed pursuit. The young man finally drove down a dead-end street and stopped. We took him out of his car to hold him for the medics to take him to the hospital. Charging him with speeding to elude the police could wait, if we decided to charge him at all. We were talking to him, and all of a sudden, he became violent and started swinging. He clipped me in the jaw. It was mild; it did not hurt, and no blood was drawn. But it sure did piss me off. While my young reflexes were not quick enough to parry that unexpected attack, they were quick enough to get my fist up, ready and able to strike back before he could stop me. His arms were down at that point, and he appeared defenseless, almost surprised at his own actions. At the last second, for reasons I still cannot explain, I chose not to strike back. Something inside me told me to stop, and I listened. Carl then grabbed him and pulled him out of my reach. I could have hit him hard, and it would have been justified, but it was just not necessary. He calmed down, and the ambulance came to take him to the hospital.

A little later, I caught up with him in the hospital just to get some information for my report. He cooperated as he periodically vomited into one of those aluminum hospital bowls. I gently reminded him that I had not charged him with the traffic offense or the more serious charge of assaulting a police officer. He thanked me, but I told him it was not charity; it was part of a deal. If he ever had a chance to make it up to me, I expected him to do so, and I did not want to have any trouble from him in the future. He agreed and continued to vomit. I left. After all, it was just another service call and I never really expected him to ever help me out.

A few months later, I was called to an apartment complex where a number of cars had been damaged in a series of hit-and-run accidents. Nobody witnessed the offending vehicle. One of the complainants did say to me that there was a party of young kids (mostly my age) going on in one of the apartments and it was getting somewhat loud and out of control. While he had not seen anything, his guess was that somebody from that party was probably responsible. I thought that was a reasonable suspicion, so I followed up on it, although I had very little, actually nothing, to go on. The apartment having the party was on the ground floor. Calling in my location on the radio, I walked towards the loud music and firmly knocked on the door. When it opened, I was met by four young men who were probably around my age. They were obviously drinking, getting rowdy, and ready for a fight. They came out of the door together and started walking towards me in unison. At that point, I realized that I had a problem and I probably should have waited for backup before making the approach. No words were even exchanged yet, but as I started backing up, one hand was on my weapon and the other was reaching for the radio to call for help. Within moments, a call came from inside the apartment telling everyone to back off. Another young man emerged from the crowd, which had moved off to the sides.

"Hi, Officer Tabman. Remember me?"

"Yes, I do." We walked into the parking lot together.

"How can I help you, Officer?"

"Well, somebody ran into a few of the cars here in the parking lot, and a number of people suspect it was someone from your party who did it. What can you tell me?"

"I can tell you that I remember how nice you were to me and that I owe you one. I did it. I hit the cars," he confessed to me.

Yes, this was the man whom we had pursued. He had struck me, and just because my gut told me to, I had let him off the hook. I had made a deal with him. Now he was paying me back. This time, I acted with the same approach. Since he confessed to me, I did not charge him with hit-and-run, as long as he agreed for me to give his name to the victims and he made good on all the repairs. He agreed. I contacted all the victims and told them that if they were not compensated to call me. The victims were very happy and probably surprised that I was able to find the culprit. When I followed up on this, I found that all victims had been compensated. This was all resolved because, while thinking on my feet, I chose not to carry out what would have been a natural, visceral reaction to a physical attack against me.

In the business world, it is, hopefully, unlikely that you will be attacked physically. But you will be attacked by sarcasm, insults, and inappropriate words, tones, and behavior. There is also another attack you will be subjected to. Who said there is no such thing as a stupid question? There are plenty of stupid questions out there. You will be bombarded with them. I think they often arise from people who are simply not paying attention or just want to voice a dissenting thought no matter what. You must be able to respond quickly and effectively to these verbal attacks. Not everyone is adept at verbal sparring; maybe you are not. At the same time, you do not want to get caught with the "deer in the headlights look" when challenged verbally, which brings up an important point: if you cannot think quickly on your feet, go for the next best thing—make it look like you are thinking on your feet. How do you that? Be prepared.

Think of all the witty responses politicians have blurted out during debates. On-the-spot humor? Hardly. These candidates studied their opponents. They knew what issues, experiences and stories would be brought up. Ronald Reagan knew the issue of his age would arise, and he was prepared with his response about his opponent's youth and inexperience. Similarly, Senator Lloyd Bentsen knew that his opponent, Dan Quayle, often cited Jack Kennedy's young age, and Bentsen was ready with his "You're no Jack Kennedy" retort, leaving Quayle almost stunned.

In this dynamic and fluid world, thinking on your feet can be incredibly effective. On September 11, 2001, the first plane struck the World Trade Center at 8:46 a.m. EST. By 9:26 a.m. EST, the FAA had halted all takeoffs and rerouted all inbound flights to the United States. That was thousands of flights. This was accomplished within less than one hour of the first crash. With all the criticism being thrown around for the events of 9/11, somebody at the FAA deserves credit for thinking on his feet. In January 2009, we watched in amazement when a veteran airline pilot was able to land a jetliner that had lost both engines safely on to the Hudson River and saved all 155 aboard.

Be confident; be bold. Execute! Whether you are stopping to think or thinking quickly on your feet, make sure you…

CHAPTER 3

Lesson: <u>Have a Measured Response</u>
Or, "Send just one agent to that bank robbery."

Besides being dynamic and fluid, we seem to be a society of extremes. Politically, our nation seems to be on balance when we are in the middle of extreme political thought or ideology. Yet in trying to get to that middle, the pendulum seems to pass right through it, swinging all the way to the left and again to the right.

Our good times are extreme as well. The roaring 1920s brought the Depression of the 1930s. The excesses of the 1990s brought us the financial meltdown starting around 2007 and hopefully climaxing by the end of 2009. Even our resolution of the problem seems excessive—a bailout costing our country trillions of dollars. The results will define this as either excessive or appropriate, but for the moment, we seem to be caught in a web of excesses. What does all this have to do with bank robberies?

A bank robbery was just the kind of crime that made legends, like Jesse James and John Dillinger. Bank robberies were also an integral ingredient in J. Edgar Hoover's FBI becoming a legendary crime-fighting organization. Unfortunately, bank robberies were good for business—at least the business of the FBI. So, why would the FBI even consider not working bank robberies anymore?

After 9/11, it was no secret—actually, it was painfully obvious—that the FBI would have to move a great deal of its resources and personnel to its counterterrorism program. As with any organization, there were finite resources. Adding to one program led to a dearth of resources in another program. In this book, we discuss the FBI's changing role and priorities after 9/11. The trend of moving away from violent crimes, drugs, and bank robberies increased incrementally each year after 2001. At a conference in 2005, the FBI director, though attempting to speak in vague terms, made it clear that he was considering completely discontinuing the FBI's involvement in bank robberies. Horrified SACs responded with the same packaged argument that had been used since 9/11. The FBI could not walk away from bank robberies—bank robberies were the FBI's history; bank robberies were great for liaison with the local police; bank robberies were great training opportunities for new agents; only the FBI could investigate the bank robbers who operated interstate; and so forth. None of these arguments lacked validity. However, those arguments did not represent the other truths—bank robberies were exciting; bank robberies were fun to work; bank robberies made for great press conferences; and bank robbery arrests drove up a field office's arrest statistics. The agents in the field wanted to work bank robberies.

By the time I retired, the FBI was still working bank robberies. In order to stay in bank robberies, FBI headquarters directed the field offices to engage in a measured response. What did that mean? Basically, for a bank robbery in which there was no shooting, hostages, or overt violence, an office would dispatch only one or two agents to work with the local police—a measured response as opposed to the full squad approach the FBI was accustomed to taking. While most field offices found ways to stay actively engaged in bank robberies, when asked by headquarters about their bank robbery program, the answer always was, "Measured response." Considering all the directives that came out of headquarters that were confusing, contradictory, or impossible to implement, this one was sound. With this measured response, the FBI was able to accomplish more than one objective—it maintained its investigative interests in bank robberies and was able to satisfy Congress and itself that the counterterrorism program would remain as top priority and not suffer from responding to bank robberies.

Reacting to any challenge or conflict with a measured response seems like an easy path towards resolution—almost a no-brainer. Yet, that just does not seem to be how we do things, especially in government and the world of politics. When we have what appears to be a crisis, Uncle Sam tends to respond with a knee-jerk reaction, usually over-responding by throwing around more money and resources than necessary, rather than thinking out an effective, efficient—and, yes, measured—response.

For example, let's look at the drug wars that the United States was getting deeply involved in around the late 1970s and early 1980s. This was truly a crisis, and the Drug Enforcement Administration (DEA) appeared to be overwhelmed, not through any fault of the agency, just due to the nature and magnitude of the problem. In 1982, President Reagan gave the FBI concurrent jurisdiction with the DEA to work drug investigations. On the surface, this was not a bad idea. Here were two very competent agencies fighting this massive war. More is better; more agents meant more success, right? Wrong. That is not to say that each agency could not or did not do a good job on its own. Unfortunately, much was lost by not considering the ramifications of this response, specifically competition for resources and the turf wars that would ensue.

When I was working narcotics in New York during the late 1980s and early 1990s, we could not work any case, short of a quick buy-bust undercover deal, where we would not bump heads with the DEA trying to target the same subject. I was assigned to an FBI-NYPD Task Force. Often, we would run into a DEA-NYPD Task Force. Even worse, because so much federal money was being thrown at drug work, everyone was trying to get in on the act. My investigations led me right into IRS operations; they claimed that drug dealers did not report their profits as income, so the IRS had jurisdiction. Or, U.S. Customs would be working the cases because the drugs were being imported and crossing our borders. If the drug dealer mailed a letter on the way to a drug deal, the postal inspectors may be there. There was constant conflict and negotiations. The ramifications of everybody attacking the same problem in different ways with different goals and conflicting motivations simply were not thought out. More does not necessarily mean better; that is just a knee-jerk reaction, not a measured response.

I did learn one hard fact from these interagency conflicts. While trying to resolve them through negotiations, the question would always be asked, usually by the prosecutor who just wanted a good case to bring to court, "Why can't you just compromise?" That was what usually wound up happening—we compromised. A compromise, while sounding reasonable, was not always the best answer, and usually proved to be a poor resolution to a conflict. A compromise had inherent problems.

Let's say the FBI was pursuing plan A, and the DEA was pursuing plan B. Each plan, on its own, probably was a good one for that particular agency's objectives and methods of operation. Choosing one plan over the other would probably achieve the mission of the investigation. Unfortunately, no agency was going to give in completely to the other agency's idea, for both practical and human nature reasons. So what did we do? We compromised and came up with plan C. Now, plan C may not have been what either agency felt was the best plan. Yet realistically, it was the only way the agencies would cooperate, allowing them to save face. From my experience, these compromises rarely, if ever, produced optimal results. Why has Congress been viewed by most Americans as completely ineffective? Does either party allow the other to implement a bill or plan on its own, or must there always be a compromise, so both parties could grab political capital? How well has that worked?

This is not to suggest that spouses, neighbors, friends, and even countries should not compromise to resolve their personal or political conflicts. For decisions that have far-reaching consequences, compromise may sound like a measured response, though it is not; it is a simple, non-confrontational resolution that may not serve the intended purpose.

The working relationship between the FBI and DEA did eventually improve. Why? After 9/11, the FBI moved away from the drug enforcement business, leaving much less to argue about. As one problem gets resolved, another arises. In an msnbc.com on-line article entitled, *'Battle of the badges' between ATF and FBI*, dated September 15, 2009, the Associated Press reported of the two agencies, "...racing each other to crime scenes, failing to share information and refusing to train together... repeated squabbles to claim jurisdiction in investigations of explosives incidents across the country..." Also noted was the transfer of ATF from the Treasury Department to the Department of Justice (where the FBI is assigned) several years ago in an effort to quell these disputes. Why would *that* work? The FBI and DEA are both under the Department of Justice – we see how well that worked out.

In 1995, the Alfred P. Murrah Federal Building in Oklahoma City was bombed in an outrageous act of domestic terrorism. I am sure all of us remember this tragic event. At the time, I was stationed in FBI headquarters. Though not involved in the investigation, I was privy to briefings on its development. While all the media pundits and self-proclaimed experts were yelling Islamic extremism, I knew that the FBI had focused in on Timothy McVeigh very early on. Shortly after this tragedy and after McVeigh, not an Islamic extremist, was arrested, everyone started screaming about the threat of domestic terrorism and the next impending and inevitable attack. So what did Congress do? A measured response? Not quite. They threw a bunch of bodies (agent positions) at the FBI to be dedicated to working domestic terrorism and nothing else. There was one problem. While domestic terrorism was a bona fide threat that the FBI needed to monitor, the FBI did not need all those agents dedicated to it. Despite this horrific act of domestic terrorism, this single tragedy did not indicate a widespread, fast-growing threat. But since Congress mandated this, the FBI had to follow it. An FBI field office would be criticized by headquarters for not using all those agent positions to work domestic terrorism, whether they needed to or not. The result was wasted resources because of a knee-jerk reaction—thinking more means better.

Again, let's revisit September 11, 2001, the most extreme tragedy of them all. The FBI quite appropriately threw most of its resources into getting to the bottom of what happened and to assure that another attack was not imminent. Not to minimize the tragedy and suffering caused by the Oklahoma City bombing, 9/11 had a new facet that made it different. The magnitude of this crime, the number of conspirators, and the international nexus made this act of terror a whole new ball game. This was an extraordinary tragedy and one for which we were just not prepared. "Measured" was probably not the type of response the FBI was striving for, nor was it one the American people were seeking. Extraordinary circumstances call for extraordinary measures, and the quest for revenge cannot be minimized or discounted. After our nation's and the FBI's initial reaction to this attack was established, the continued response in the ensuing years was not an appropriate measured response. In the field offices throughout the country, the FBI was dedicating significant numbers of agents to counterterrorism more for appearance than necessity. All SACs were feeling pressured to assure the director that they were fighting counterterrorism, the FBI's number-one priority, with everything they had. But that was not proving effective and efficient.

During my tenure, I saw terrorism cases opened on Muslims who were committing petty crimes, ones that the FBI would probably never otherwise investigate and where there was little evidence or indication to suggest a nexus to terrorism. There existed a hesitancy to close these cases, as agents were afraid that they might be wrong; what if the subject was later implicated in a terrorist plot? The targets of these investigations paid a price. They were put on watch lists and then had difficulties when traveling or seeking citizenship. Misuses of the PATRIOT Act regarding the issuance of National Security Letters were becoming commonplace in the FBI. These letters were demands for certain information such as toll records, which the FBI used in terrorism investigations. The pressure of the FBI's response to terrorism was challenging the FBI's abilities to protect and respect civil rights. In March 2007 and again in March 2008, the Department of Justice, Office of the Inspector General released reports that cited FBI misuses of National Security Letters. Though the FBI was able to cite improvements in its processes for managing National Security Letters, the report ignited the debate of just how much freedom were we willing to surrender in the name of national security.

There had to be adequate predication for these letters to be issued, at least some reasonable connection to terrorism. The requests I was getting to sign these letters did not always present such justification. When I implemented new procedures that required that the agents justify the requests for the National Security Letters, surprisingly, I was met with great resistance from the agents, though what I was asking for was consistent with the PATRIOT Act. The FBI was now implementing an unmeasured response—one that was causing the FBI to violate the very principles and rights it was sworn to protect.

This is not to say that the FBI did not have success stories in their counterterrorism efforts. They have put together some good cases, and good cases deserved credit, but unmeasured responses to their success—or perceived success—had consequences. In Miami in June 2006, the FBI arrested seven individuals for planning terrorist attacks at numerous sites including the Sears Tower. However, the message of success that the FBI and Department of Justice tried to communicate may have been lost due to their over-reaction to these arrests. The attorney general personally held a press conference to announce the arrests. Generally, such arrests were announced publicly by the local FBI office and the United States Attorney's Office. The attorney general personally making the announcement clearly sent a message that this was a really big 9/11-esque case. While watching the press conference and listening to the reporters' questions and tones, it became obvious that the media was not impressed. Taken from Wikipedia, this is a snippet of the press conference:

> **Question:** Did any of the men have any actual contact with any members of al-Qaeda that you know of?
>
> **Attorney-General:** The answer to that is "No".
>
> **Question:** Did they have any means to carry out this plot? I mean, did you find any explosives, weapons?
>
> **Attorney-General:** You raise a good point... We took action when we had enough evidence.
>
> **Question:** Was there anything against the Sears Tower other than this one apparent, just, kind of mention of the Sears Tower? It doesn't look like they ever took pictures or...
>
> **Deputy Director of the FBI:** One of the individuals was familiar with the Sears Tower, had

worked in Chicago, and was familiar with the tower. But in terms of the plans, it was more aspirational than operational.

Originally, one defendant had been acquitted and the other six defendants had two mistrials declared. In May 2009, five of the defendants were convicted and one was acquitted. While reading coverage of the conviction, many reports focused on the fact that it took three attempts and almost three years to bring this case to conclusion, not that it was a successful investigation. Was this the right case for the attorney general to announce personally?

In June 2007, the FBI arrested individuals allegedly engaged in a plot to ignite a jet fuel pipeline running through JFK Airport in Queens, New York, and the adjacent neighborhoods. Clearly, this was a scary possibility, and that point was driven home via a press conference held jointly by the United States Attorney's Office, the FBI, and the New York City Police Department. Surprisingly, shortly after the plot was announced, the public response did not seem to be one of relief that it was uncovered at an early stage. Instead, many experts came forward to explain why the plot never would have worked and how these suspects, once again, did not have the wherewithal to pull this plot off. The media stressed that the plot, after at least one year of investigation, was still in the planning stages. The involvement of an FBI informant with something to gain was put into question. This does not negate the legitimacy of the investigation. The FBI was in receipt of information that individuals were planning a terrorist attack, and they had to investigate. The ability or inability to succeed in their plot was almost irrelevant to the fact that they were planning a terrorist attack. The mere plotting of such an attack was illegal and the FBI could not take the slightest risk that the plot would reach fruition. Yet, the public and the media did not appear impressed.

So, why did these cases come under such scrutiny and question rather than receive accolades? When cases were publicized as bigger than they really were, using fear as a political and promotional tool, the public and the press became wary and the legitimate efforts of the law enforcement community were undermined. Perhaps a more measured claim of success would have brought a more measured media response. In contrast, in September 2009, the FBI appeared to have averted a significant terrorist plot. This time the media responded more positively.

From 2003 through 2004, while the FBI focused so strongly on terrorism cases, such as the ones above, I spoke to numerous United States attorneys throughout the country who all bemoaned the dwindling number of criminal cases the FBI was bringing to them while producing very questionable results in terrorism. Certain FBI field offices were reporting increases in mortgage fraud—a foreboding of the crisis in 2009. Organized crime was reinventing itself. Nobody questioned the need of the FBI to make terrorism a priority, but not at the expense of everything else. Many wondered if the FBI would be able to maintain its primary jurisdiction over so many criminal offenses if it could not develop an appropriate response to many challenges simultaneously. I was not surprised when a colleague of mine forwarded to me a November 2006 article from a West Coast newspaper stating that the Justice Department had refused to prosecute 87 percent of international terrorism cases brought by the FBI from October 2005 through June 2006. The pressure of producing results was leading to FBI offices putting together weak terrorism cases while other threats were not receiving adequate attention, the results of an unmeasured response.

By late 2007, the FBI appeared to be moving back to the middle. Arrests of mobsters were announced. White-collar crime investigations of major financial firms and mortgage fraud investigations were making the news. By 2009, in the midst of the economic meltdown, the FBI announced a plan to "fast track" white-collar crimes. If the FBI does not find a measured response to its numerous competing priorities, it is very possible that Congress will refine and redefine the FBI and its mission.

On September 11, 2006, I held a local press conference to discuss the FBI's counterterrorism efforts since September 11, 2001. The next day, the headline of the article in the local newspaper read, "FBI Has Two Terrorism Squads." Though I knew that having a second squad did not really tell the story, I also knew the headline would play well; my media rep was pleased. We are a society impressed by numbers. Sometimes numbers reflect the bottom line; sometimes they blur the bottom line.

In their book *Greed and Corporate Failure*, authors Stewart Hamilton and Alicia Micklethwait referred to the Sarbanes-Oxley Act, a law enacted in 2002 to set additional standards for matters such as financial reporting, corporate governance, auditing and accountability as, "...a knee jerk response to events, which was rushed through Congress in a matter of four months." Many others view the act as necessary in the post Enron, WorldCom world. I did find it interesting that the authors considered legislation drafted in response to a crisis to be a knee-jerk response. I wonder what their reaction would have been to the Troubled Asset Relief Program signed by President George W. Bush and the following American Recovery and Reinvestment Act of 2009 signed by President Obama.

Maybe it takes a crisis to start seeing the big picture. When do we start worrying about our dependency on foreign oil? Only during an energy crisis. How many times have we discussed the issue and then it was forgotten? When do we worry about an unfriendly nation? Only when they start flexing their muscle. After the Cold War, we turned our attention away from Russia, but they are back baring their claws. China, Iran, and North Korea slowly drifted into our radar while we focused on Iraq. Even Afghanistan seemed to have gotten lost and now requires a new focus.

Response to a crisis must be swift and bold, but it must also be measured. If you drop everything else, you have responded to, but have not managed the crisis. You have put out one fire while allowing another spark to ignite. Undoubtedly, you will at some time, if not numerous times, be confronted by some type of unusual crisis in your business. Perhaps it will be a product recall or a surprise move by a competitor that calls for a response. Maybe you will be at risk from an intellectual property theft or major industrial accident. Perhaps you will experience media leaks that are harmful to your company. There were many media leaks within the FBI. These leaks are dangerous and frustrating, and you will want to plug the leaks immediately. Once again, an overreaction can cause you more trouble than the original problem.

Ask Hewlett Packard about their response to media leaks. In September 2006, Hewlett Packard found that its long-term strategy had been leaked to the media. Clearly, this would be a crisis for any firm, but especially for one in such a highly competitive market. Chairwoman Patricia Dunn decided to conduct an internal investigation, which became more of a spying mission. Business and personal e-mail and telephone records of the ten other directors were obtained through questionable methods. The leak was identified. However, Dunn resigned and later faced criminal charges. She was bold and decisive, and tried to protect the company. We must ask if this was measured response, or did she suffer from shooting from the hip? In March 2007, all charges against Patricia Dunn were dropped.

There are numerous challenges that a business may encounter that will require a quick, bold, and public response. You can move quickly and decisively without shooting from the hip. Have a crisis plan and a crisis management team. You will need input from the various entities of your company to get the full picture of what may be the effects of your response; each such entity should be represented by someone on the crisis management team. Do you have a method to identify employees who have valuable expertise obtained in school or from previous employment, which they are not using now, but would be valuable to managing the crisis?

Though this sounds counterintuitive, you may have to slow down a bit, just to make sure your responses have been given adequate thought and consideration. Assign someone to be a devil's advocate, again, just to assure you are not moving too hastily. If, during a time of crisis or at a critical juncture in an organization's existence, leadership appears to be in panic mode, in a bunker mentality locked behind closed doors, the message is to keep quiet and just wait for the next directive from executive management. Such a message does not engender creative thought or intellectual dialogue that may help to resolve the crisis.

Listen to your mother: when you are mad, count to ten before you speak. Shooting from the hip will create crises. By having a measured response to a potential crisis, you will be begin to…

CHAPTER 4

Lesson: <u>Manage Risks</u>
Or, "This arrest plan does not address all my
concerns. Let's rethink this."

By 2009, with the economic crisis full blown, foreclosures at record numbers, joblessness rising to scary rates, and stocks at ten-year lows, the word *risk* had become commonplace if not hackneyed. Do we bail out banks and corporations that took unacceptable risks? Do we save the homes of those who took risky mortgages? Risk transcended all professions and all aspects of life.

Risk in the business world generally falls into three categories. First is market risk. As the name implies, this represents the risk of the value of investments based upon movements in the markets. Market risks can be further subdivided into four risk factors: equity risk, interest rate risk, currency risk, and commodity risk. The less you know about these, probably the safer you are. A little knowledge can be a dangerous thing.

The next risk is credit risk, which, also as the name implies, is the risk that debts cannot be paid. The inability of so many Americans to meet their mortgage obligations led to the housing crisis and other related financial crises during 2008 and 2009. This risk was probably on the minds of most Americans during this time.

In 1983, I reported to the FBI Oklahoma City Field Office, a rookie agent fresh out of the FBI Academy. One investigation consumed the office: Penn Square Bank. Penn Square Bank, located in Oklahoma City, had engaged in irresponsible energy loans during the oil boom years. When the boom petered out, Penn Square and many of the banks to whom they had sold loans were left with millions of dollars of loan write-offs. Irresponsible lending practices—sound familiar? More than twenty-five years later, it looks like we have not really learned our lessons. Then and now, we have credit risk to the max.

The third category of risk is operational risk. Operational risk, in simple terms, is everything else—the risks that arise simply from existing. These risks can be the slip and falls, product recalls, poor customer service, or any event that subjects you to liability or may harm your reputation. Minimizing the possibility of being harmed by these risks is the art and science of risk management.

How can you manage your risks without knowing what your risks are? In the days following 9/11, I, and I am sure many of my colleagues, received telephone calls from local business owners and community leaders asking for a meeting. They all wanted to discuss—no surprise—security. What can we do to protect ourselves?

The first question I would ask was, "What are you trying to protect against?" The answer was, naturally,

terrorism. OK, but what about terror? Terror encom-
passes numerous possibilities. In view of the 9/11 attacks,
were businesses hoping to protect themselves from an
airplane attack? Nothing here is meant to diminish the
pain our country experienced or to be disrespectful to
the victims and their families, but the reality was that the
possibility of such an attack was a risk that we all had to
live with. Identifying and weighing risk, otherwise known
as risk assessment, is an integral step in protecting our
businesses and assets.

Each business has its own particular risks. Let's look
at the risks of police work. Those are obvious, or so we
think. Making arrests and stopping suspicious people are
inherently dangerous tasks. These risks, while they cannot
be avoided, are managed by training. Risks are also managed
by setting policies that help minimize risk. Despite what you
see on television, police officers do not offer themselves as
hostages in exchange for civilian hostages. A police officer
will not remove his gun and raise his hands to a gunman
saying, "Look, I'm unarmed." Those are unnecessary risks
and are tantamount to negligent police work. Yet there are
other risks that are not quite as obvious.

Are arrests really the most significant threat to a
police officer, or are they just the most obvious? In reality, a police officer is more likely to die of heart disease
than through the violent act of an assailant. What about
the mental health of our law enforcement personnel? Is
that a significant risk? Stress begins to take its toll on the

strongest of us. Again, we tend to think of stress as emanating from dangerous situations or irregular hours. Nevertheless, the day-to-day workplace environment can be a source of tremendous stress—yes, even in your place of business and even in the FBI.

An inspection I once conducted of a major FBI field office found that the SAC was brutal in the use of his authority. He liked to screw with people for the fun of it. He was mean and vindictive. During the interviews of the office personnel, we found a major problem with stress. I personally spoke to senior agents who were on the verge of tears because of the treatment they were receiving from the SAC. The inspection team wound up making several mandatory referrals to our Employee Assistance Program. That was not good. I am glad we came when we did and were able to help. One question we did not answer: where was the rest of the management team in that office? While they were subordinate to the SAC, they were also responsible for monitoring the well-being of their agents. They should have made those referrals and let the SAC know that several agents were experiencing severe stress. There was no indication that had happened. Low morale and dislike of managers was not uncommon in the FBI, and I imagine in many corporate environments. I have been on both sides of that equation. Requiring Employee Assistance Program intervention raised the issue to a dangerous level.

So what if our personnel are unhappy and stressed? So what if an FBI agent is experiencing stress at the workplace?

Aren't they trained to deal with stress? Well, yes and no. Facing danger on your own terms is one thing; feeling personally persecuted, disrespected and underappreciated by your employer is another. What is the risk of agents under severe stress? First, would you want an agent whose mind is not clear backing you up on an arrest? He may mean well but will not have the perspicacity needed to perform as expected. That is not the only risk. While almost all agents are honest, the FBI has had some agents turn against our country and commit espionage. I do not profess to know their motives, but I do believe if pushed too far, anyone, even an honest FBI agent, can become so stressed and so unhappy that revenge becomes his only outlet.

Do you really want to push an employee that far? By failing to know your employees on a basic level, unable to recognize changes in their behavior, and not to treat them with a certain modicum of respect and decency is to invite risks. You want to minimize and control the risks to your business, not create an environment that fosters risk.

In early 2009, workplace and domestic violence dominated the headlines. In recent months, I have given several presentations and interviews relative to the increasing risk of workplace violence as the worsening economy is causing job losses and threats to many people's livelihoods.

Not all risks are as dramatic or attention grabbing as workplace violence. One of the best examples of risk management came from a sergeant of mine when I was a young officer on patrol. We were in roll call, and he said, "Don't."

He was answering his own question that he posed for the squad. It was a very snowy, icy night. He asked, "What is the best way to drive on a night like this?" Then he gave that answer. Knowing that a patrol car could not remain stagnant, he went on to remind us that when we did drive, just keep a healthy distance from any other vehicles and drive only as fast as the weather permitted. When we got on the streets, I asked my partner what we were supposed to do if there was an emergency call and we could not drive more than 10 or 15 miles an hour because of the weather.

He answered, "Then you drive 10 or 15 miles an hour." That proved to be a rather obvious answer that rendered my question as extremely stupid. Not being able to drive full speed to an emergency call just seemed counterintuitive to a rookie cop. Reality is such that life is imperfect. Putting ourselves and others at risk by speeding on ice, even in the face of an emergency, created more risk; it did not reduce it. Despite an impending emergency, the situation dictated a measured response. When I stopped and thought about it, I realized just what a simple concept that was.

Risk can come in many forms, some are obvious and some are rather subtle. Financial risk is naturally an overwhelming major concern to businesses, even without thinking about the economic crisis in 2009. Although I am a CPA, one look at my stock portfolio will make you quickly understand why I do not give financial risk advice. However, there are simple operational rules that should be followed when it comes to your money, such as separation of duties, appropriate levels of approval authority, accountability, audit trails to trace transactions to people or events, and scheduled and unscheduled reconciliations of accounts.

Risks come from both internal and external factors. The risks can be political, environmental, or related to a specific project. That project may require its own dedicated risk management efforts. Your other business risks may include supply chain interruption, competition, defective products, and perhaps inadequate insurance. Have you considered how crime may be a risk to your business? Not the typical muggings or street crime, though those are real dangers, but I am discussing crime more in the form of organized crime and public corruption.

In the mid 1980s, the FBI conducted one of its most famous Mafia prosecutions in what was known as the Commission Trial. The top bosses of the Mafia's five main families in New York were all convicted on racketeering charges. The most infamous was perhaps Paul Costellano of the Gambino crime family; he was murdered under the orders of John Gotti before he went to trial. Also prosecuted were Anthony Salerno of the Genovese crime family, Carmine Persico of the Colombo crime family, Anthony Corallo of the Lucchese crime family, and Philip Rastelli of the Bonanno crime family. How did this affect business? A federal prosecutor friend of mine, who successfully prosecuted John Gotti, told me that shortly after these convictions, the cost of cement dropped significantly in New York City. No cement shoe jokes. Mob control of the cement industry and thus of the construction business was well known. Just as an aside: Carmine Persico decided to go pro se, which means he acted as his own attorney. I was in court one day when he was attempting to cross-examine a family member (crime family and true relative) who had decided to cooperate with the government. It was really quite entertaining to see them verbally spar as adversaries after having been literally partners in some horrendous crimes.

A friend of mine once worked for a trucking company in New York that moved freight from the airport. As the business manager, she asked her boss why none of the trucks were marked with the company's name and logo; there was no identification of the company and, thus, no advertising. She found this rather unusual as most trucks had their company name prominently displayed. Her boss had a very simple answer. He did not want the mob to notice him and all the business he was doing at the airport. The airport was known to be "their territory," and he was not looking to take them on. Good risk management? I certainly thought so. It was an unfortunate fact, but that was reality.

Another eye-opener to the effect organized crime had on business I experienced when I was a young agent newly assigned to New York City. Through an investigation I was working on, I met a young gentleman about my age who had been successful in the construction and rehabilitation business in New York City. He would bid on rehabilitating buildings that the city had condemned. He also owned a number of apartment buildings and made significant money as a landlord. While we were talking over dinner, he explained his process of collecting and accounting for his rent money. Pointing out what I thought were several deficiencies in the process he was describing, I could see he was getting nervous at what I was suggesting. We quickly finished dinner and went back to his office to follow up on my suspicions. After looking in desk drawers, under cabinets, and in other such places, he found thousands of dollars stashed and hidden all over the office with no accompanying paperwork.

A few weeks later, he called to tell me that he had fired that employee, and tens of thousands of dollars could not be accounted for and would probably never be recovered. I offered some suggestions as to how to improve the process, one was as simple as generating a copy of each receipt for rent collected. He had not done that and therefore could never reconcile rents received versus money deposited. He liked my ideas and then offered me a job.

He offered to triple what I was making at the FBI, which was not too hard to do for a private firm. Willing to consider this lucrative offer, I met him again at a later date to discuss the details. He wanted to hire me to help run his operations and assure that he was not getting ripped off by his employees and to generally run the business effectively and efficiently. He told me, though, that he had one serious concern with me. He did not want me to be an FBI agent anymore. I had to leave that part of my life behind. What he was telling me was that he had people on his payroll who never did any work. Big, burly guys would show up periodically, and he would give them envelopes full of cash. No discussions, no questions asked. He was paying off the mob so he could continue to do business in New York City.

"Can you live with that?" he asked me. He did not want me to challenge it, report it, or interfere with the process in any way. That was business in New York City at the time, and he was willing to live with it. It did not take much time for me to make a decision. I realized that I could not live with that, and I declined a rather tempting offer. He managed risk for both of us simply by communicating the truth. And I am sure we both made the right decision, for ourselves.

Public corruption is also a business risk that most people do not even recognize. It is so insidious, cloaked by collusion of willing parties, that you do not even know it is happening, and you do not know what it is costing you. My first realization about the personal impact of public corruption came about the same time as the above story, when I was a young agent in New York City. I was dating a girl who lived in Manhattan. We were just walking around the city, and she pointed out a certain building to me. She and her ex-husband used to own a restaurant there, she told me. They loved the business but sold out. I asked if they were forced to sell in order to settle the divorce. No, that was not it. She explained how the cops would come by and shake them down for cash payments. Health inspectors and firefighters would come by for either cash or bottles of champagne or buckets of shrimp. If any of them walked out empty-handed, the restaurant was cited for all sorts of safety and health violations, which would get very costly. Eventually, the demands got so great that the restaurant could not sustain profitability, despite the fact that these costs had to be passed on to the customers.

This story was not a condemnation of cops, firefighters, or health inspectors. It was just one story told to me more than twenty years ago. I am confident this did not represent a majority of these dedicated civil servants, and I am equally confident things in New York City have changed, for the better, over the years. This story was just another example of one of those pesky little risks we do not always think about.

Public Corruption was the top priority of the FBI Criminal Program. These cases were tough to investigate. Consider that generally there were two willing parties, colluding to break the law in a very secretive way. Unlike a bank robbery, we often did not know a crime had even occurred. Getting to the bottom of the problem, or actually, just scratching the surface of it, required "beating the bushes" – talking to people who may have information, such as contractors or even other politicians. Basically, we were trying to develop informants. When I would give speeches about our office's public corruption plan, I would talk about it in two ways. First, the good news: the plan worked. Second, the bad news: the plan worked. We opened a number of cases and had successful prosecutions of local politicians.

At the heart of the corruption problem were construction contracts, bid rigging, and zoning.

The reality of how quickly time had passed occurred when I was giving a speech to a group of local prosecutors about public corruption. I discussed the seminal public corruption investigation known as ABSCAM from the late 1970s into the early 1980s. The blank look on many faces showed me just how fast the years had passed. ABSCAM was an FBI undercover operation that began initially as a stolen property investigation but morphed into a public corruption case. The FBI set up a fictitious company with employees posing as Middle Eastern businessmen. These businessmen offered money to government officials in return for political favors. In the end, several federal and local politicians were convicted of bribery-related crimes. Just as September 11 traumatically exposed us to the new threat of terrorism, ABSCAM was the wake-up call to the threat of public corruption.

Not quite as intriguing as organized crime and public corruption, there are operational risks in the form of physical dangers—an elevator that has shown signs of malfunction, wires strung across a floor causing people to trip, or a multitude of other such problems. Obviously, there is a moral obligation to fix these problems and protect your employees. As well, failure to take timely corrective action can result in serious liability. Other risks may not be as clearly defined as physical danger. Failure to enforce rules, regulations, or laws could put a business at risk. Recent corporate events contributing to the financial meltdown of 2008 and 2009 have proven that true. Inadequate training of employees or ignoring employee misconduct raises the level of risk.

The insurance industry also refers to risks posed by moral hazards—where people do not make the right ethical choices. Sometimes, ethical issues are very clear; sometimes they are more clouded. One poignant example I recall was back in the mid to late 1990s when I was a supervisor at FBI headquarters. The investigation of the Oklahoma City bombing had been concluded. I noticed on someone's desk what looked like a rock that had been engraved with the employee's name and recognition of the work the employee did on the investigation. It looked like a nice award, and I commented on it. The employee told me that this "rock" was actually a piece of rubble from the Murrah Federal Building, which had been destroyed by the bomb. The FBI had collected this rubble and turned the pieces into mementos for those who worked on the investigation.

On the surface, this seemed like a harmless idea to acknowledge the efforts of those who worked through an emotionally trying investigation. Even so, I started to think, was that rubble the property of the FBI? Did the FBI really have the right to take that and turn it over to employees for personal use? Wasn't that act of giving the rubble as some sort of gift suggesting that the rubble had some intrinsic value? I casually mentioned my concerns to some of my colleagues and even my supervisor. Getting sarcastic remarks in return, I was assured that I was over thinking the matter, as I am often accused of doing. Years passed, and the issue was never raised. Had I given this matter too much thought? Perhaps; that would not be unlike me.

Fast-forward to September 11, 2001. Once again, the crime scene left rubble to be collected. The emotions of the investigation were as strong as the Oklahoma City bombing, if not stronger. As with the Oklahoma City bombing, such rubble and remnants of personal belongings wound up in the personal possession of FBI agents. The issue came to light with the "Tiffany globe" affair. An agent at ground zero found a small Tiffany globe in the rubble at the scene. Clearly, it had been sitting on someone's desk before the tragedy, and realistically, the owner would probably not be identified and the globe probably not returned to a family member. The agent took the globe into his personal possession and brought it back to his home office. The globe found its way onto the agent's secretary's desk. No thought was given to this until another agent of that office raised it as an ethical issue and this caught the attention of the media. Receiving very negative press coverage, the FBI subsequently acknowledged that agents had removed items from ground zero and kept them as personal mementos, but was quick to point out that these agents broke no rules. Eventually, the FBI enacted a new policy prohibiting such collection of items from a crime scene.

We should recognize that no FBI agent tried to make money or any other personal gain from these mementos.

Even so, how could the FBI have failed to see this coming? When were law enforcement agents ever allowed to take potential evidence, personal belongings, or any item from the scene of a crime and convert it to personal use? In the volumes of rules in the FBI, how could there be no rule addressing this possibility? Though these actions did not affect the outcome of any investigation, they could have. This tarnished the image of the FBI as an agency beyond reproach in matters of ethics, though it was short-lived, as FBI successes far outnumbered such incidents. This was a vivid example of a failure to identify a moral risk and take corrective action. The best way to manage and minimize risk is to see it coming and stop it dead in its tracks. Do you have a process for identifying potential risks? Is risk management integrated into the operations of your business? Enterprise risk management has become a buzzword in 2009 as we have been overwhelmed by the consequences of poor corporate risk management.

After almost twenty-four years in the FBI and having served as an inspector in charge for two years, it did not take much to realize that the FBI had problems in its handling of informants, a very risky process. An inspection was a performance audit of an FBI field division, business unit by business unit, file by file, and employee by employee. They were thorough, intense and very intimidating. The inspector in charge, sometimes referred to as the inspector, had final decision-making authority and was responsible for the staff, which could number from approximately thirty to over one hundred agents and support personnel. Inspections high-lighted problems that were pervasive throughout the FBI.

One major case of espionage involved a male FBI agent having an inappropriate relationship with a female informant. An FBI agent was operating a female Chinese informant who was supposedly spying for the FBI against the Chinese intelligence services. As it turned out, the FBI agent was not operating her as an informant; she was operating the FBI agent, for the benefit of the Chinese intelligence services. The handling agent and the female Chinese informant engaged in an intimate personal relationship. The relationship went on for quite a while, and apparently, there were signs of danger that were not addressed. Let me first emphasize that I do not have any inside information on this matter. I only know what was covered in the media. But, from what I have seen over twenty-four years, I can take an educated guess as to how this was allowed to happen. The FBI was probably afraid to give any scrutiny to what appeared to be a successful undercover operation. The FBI believed the female informant was giving them valuable intelligence, and the attitude, I suspect, was probably, "Let's leave it alone; it's working fine." I say that because I saw that all too often in the FBI.

There was another well-known espionage case where an FBI agent turned traitor, which was the subject of a movie. Though an informant was not involved, it is worth mentioning. In 2001, Robert Hanssen, a senior FBI Agent was arrested and convicted for spying for Russia. During his years as an FBI agent and Russian spy, he maintained a personal relationship with a stripper, buying her expensive items such as jewelry and a Mercedes. He also had her escort him on a business trip to Hong Kong. By all accounts, the relationship was strictly platonic as he was a dedicated family man. I do not know if that fact makes this matter more or less bizarre. With Hanssen, however, his indiscretion appears to have been a byproduct of his espionage, not the motivating factor. Yet, here we find two FBI Agents who have betrayed their country and ruined their lives, and in both cases, an inappropriate relationship with a woman somehow figures in. Are we surprised?

In the June 2008 edition of the Journal of Consumer Research, on-line excerpt from an article focusing on mens' behavior, entitled *Bikinis Instigate Generalized Impatience in Intertemporal Choice,* by Bram Van den Bergh, Siegfried Dewitte and Luk Warlop states in part, "…exposure to 'hot stimuli' from one domain may thus affect decisions in a different domain. We show that exposure to sexy cues leads to more impatience in intertemporal choice between monetary rewards." Let's put this in simple terms: Men—when it comes to women and sex we make stupid decisions. Now, does knowing that reduce the risks?

Both those FBI agents operated for a significant period of time before being caught. As I opined earlier, probably because things seemed to be working, no extra scrutiny of their performance was ever given. You can take the approach of "if it ain't broke, don't fix it." That may have been a good thought to consider before Coke introduced the

New Coke. While that philosophy does have some applications, it does so only to a certain point. No operation or business practice should be free from review or assessment, no matter how successful it may appear on the surface, with *appear* being the key word. If you do not monitor and review your processes, you cannot identify potential risk factors.

The FBI has had a number of high-profile problems related to the handling of informants. In 1999, an FBI informant known as Whitey Bulger became a top-ten fugitive charged with racketeering. Also charged with racketeering was the FBI agent who had been operating Bulger as an informant. Apparently, the agent became too close to Bulger and started giving Bulger sensitive information, including Bulger's pending indictment, which led Bulger to go on the lam.

The FBI experienced another high-profile problem related to the handling of informants. One of my former supervisors from an organized crime squad was arrested and prosecuted for complicity in mob murders. Briefly, he was accused of feeding information to an informant he was handling, approximately twenty years ago, which led to that informant having certain individuals killed. The supervisor was eventually acquitted, but one could only imagine what his life must have been like going through this ordeal. This simply highlights just how fraught with danger the handling of informants can be and serves as an example of a high-risk process that requires definitive risk management.

Knowing that informants were high risk, our team developed a plan whereby certain criteria present with an informant received extra scrutiny. While the FBI had a rather decent plan for reviewing informant files, there absolutely was room for improvement. The first factor requiring extra scrutiny was when the agent and informant were of opposite genders. Now, many female agents operated male informants. We were not quite as concerned about female agents for the reasons pointed out in the article discussed above. Given today's litigious environment, we did not want to appear discriminatory. Clearly, we were most concerned with the male agent–female informant relationship. For reasons of security, I will not mention what other controls we implemented or what other factors we considered high risk, but we identified the risks and took action to address them. Foolproof? No, nothing is. We cannot eliminate risk, just like the best police department in the world cannot eliminate crime. But we can control it. Do you have a high-risk but necessary process in your business that requires extraordinary oversight? Are you providing that additional scrutiny?

Why do we seem to take risks that subsequently appear as unnecessary, and even stupid, after the damage has been done? One reason, and probably the primary reason, is that we usually get through the risk-taking activity without incident. Concurring with this thought is author Dietrich Dorner in his book *The Logic of Failure*. In discussing the Chernobyl disaster, Dorner points out that the disaster was not a result of errors or failures as generally defined, but was the result of "violations of safety rules... by no means committed here for the first time." Dorner also states, "...breaking safety rules is usually reinforced... it pays off." Because we get away with it so often, and avoid the hassle of the rule, we are tempted to keep breaking that rule. With each occurrence, the odds begin to favor failure, not success.

A great example of taking a risk one too many times is the very common running a red ("It was still yellow, Officer") light. How often have you done that? If you are one of the lucky ones who can claim nothing happened, then you will probably do it again. If you are one of the many unlucky ones I saw in just two years on patrol, then you will not take that risk again. The consequences are just too dire. So many people are asking themselves, "Why didn't I just stop for that light?" Do not become one of those people. Weigh your risk/reward ratio. Most of the little, stupid risks we take in life just are not worth it for the one time it does not turn out as expected.

Do you have a system by which risks are identified? If one area of your business seems to be more risk vulnerable than others, ask why. Is it a personnel issue, process weakness, or physical vulnerability? Have a plan for addressing the risk before a problem arises. If you do not have a system to identify and manage risk, develop one. A risk assessment followed by corrective action, then followed by the development of a crisis response plan and crisis response team should minimize risks and dangers. Today's buzzwords in this area are business continuity plans, data back-up, disaster recovery, and secondary off-sites.

There are always the small, subtle risks that you will not be aware of until after there is a problem. By being engaged with the daily operations of your business, you should pick up on these risks. Surprise audits are a great way to manage risk. An audit does not necessarily infer a financial audit. Sometimes I would just pull files at random and look through them. Although supervisors reviewed (or were supposed to review) files every ninety days, I would take an occasional glance. Looking through the files, I would find occasional problems, such as procedural deficiencies or investigations that were going nowhere. I can tell you, my subordinates did not like the idea of the boss looking through their files; too bad. These files were not theirs; they belonged to the FBI. Doing these reviews periodically, as time allowed, probably kept us out of a certain amount of administrative trouble.

One time, I did a surprise audit of all the firearms in the evidence vault. I compared the list of weapons against certain paperwork and procedures that were to be followed prior to submitting a weapon into evidence. I found 90 percent noncompliance. There was a simple fix. We implemented a policy whereby weapons would not be accepted into the evidence vault without proof that procedures were followed and paperwork completed. An audit nine months later showed 100 percent compliance.

In March 2007, I read an article in a local newspaper that described how an internal audit uncovered an embezzlement of more than $250,000, which was perpetrated by stealing truckloads of scrap metal. Surprise audits are a good thing.

Actually just minutes before writing this chapter, I observed some effective, though hardly noticeable, risk management. Yesterday, the temperature hit 70 degrees as it had been for the past week, although it was nearing the end of November. Today, while I was at a fast-food restaurant, a light rain quickly turned into a hailstorm, and the streets quickly iced up. Within minutes, the manager was out pouring salt on the walkways. He was not caught off guard by the unseasonably warm weather or quick change of circumstances. As simple as this sounds, this quick and easy task considerably reduced the risk of injury and liability.

As I mentioned earlier, starting on September 12, 2001, many law enforcement officials were being called to all sorts of facilities to discuss security. "How can we protect ourselves better?" business executives would ask. When I asked what they were trying to protect themselves from, they could not answer. They did not really anticipate a massive terrorist attack on the scale of 9/11, but the fear generated from the attacks led them to believe that they were remiss in their security planning. You must know your endgame to plan accordingly. Do not assume to know what your risks are; there are many risks lurking sub rosa. Conduct a risk assessment and identify the most likely and most dangerous risks. Failure to manage risk will result in a lot of crisis management. Avoiding crises is the goal of risk management. Risks can be reduced and knee-jerk reactions and crisis modes kept to a minimum if you take the time to…

CHAPTER 5

Lesson: <u>Watch for the Red Flags</u>
Or, "The system was blinking red."

The above quote can be attributed to George Tenet, a former director of the Central Intelligence Agency. He was referring to intelligence activities in the months immediately preceding 9/11. By reading the numerous reports, investigations, and analyses of the events leading up to 9/11, one may conclude that there were plenty of indications that a number of warning signs were present. A lack of interagency coordination and cooperation and maybe even disbelief contributed to our collective failure to take more decisive, preventive action. Of course, we will never know if we could have stopped the 9/11 attacks, and trying to place blame serves no purpose; however, after-action critiques are vital if we are to learn from our mistakes.

Shortly after retiring, I was hired by a successful businessman to investigate a series of unauthorized (i.e. fraudulent) transfers from his bank account amounting to approximately $200,000. The transfers were tracked to other accounts, the perpetrator identified, and fraud firmly established. My client wanted his money back. My client's bank, however, refunded only those transactions that fell within the preceding sixty days of his notification. This was consistent with the Electronic Fund Transfer Act, which mandated that a consumer notify the bank of a fraudulent transfer within sixty days of occurrence—not within sixty days of learning of the fraud. My client is now involved in litigation with the bank, which he may win, even though he did not make timely notification. The bank had absolutely no system of red flags alerting to this fraud. An account which never had any transfers suddenly experienced numerous and frequent transfers of high-dollar amounts. Money was floating out the door, and the bank did not take notice. They did not see the system blinking red.

In November 2008, the Federal Trade Commission enacted the Red Flag Rules. In short, these rules required financial institutions to develop a system to identify the warning signs of identity theft. Here are some of those red flags:

- Documents provided for identification appearing altered or forged

- Photograph on ID inconsistent with appearance of customer

- Application appearing forged or altered or destroyed and reassembled

- Information on ID not matching any address in the consumer report; Social Security number has not been issued or appears on the Social Security Administration's Death Master File

- Suspicious addresses supplied, such as a mail drop or prison, or phone numbers associated with pagers or answering service

- Drastic change in payment patterns, use of available credit, or spending patterns

- An account that has been inactive for a lengthy time suddenly exhibits unusual activity

We are probably thinking the same thing. Doesn't this seem a little obvious, especially for our financial institutions?

Most business losses due to theft and fraud are perpetrated from the inside and when the fraud triangle is present: motive, opportunity and rationalization. The motive can be anything from fear of job loss, demotion, cut in pay, disrespect (real or imagined), disciplinary action or denied opportunity. Many of those motives fall under the rubric of revenge. Opportunity speaks for itself. Unsupervised or unaudited access to cash and intellectual property are examples of opportunity. Rationalization can be "I deserve it," "They deserve it," or "I'll pay this back," How do you minimize the risks of fraud and internal theft? You look for the red flags:

- Accounting irregularities
- Inventory shortages
- Management overrides of polices and internal controls
- Employee behavioral changes—staying late, coming in early
- Changes in employee lifestyle
- Actual or attempted access to unauthorized files or information
- Inquiries absent a "need to know"
- Unexplained revenue shortages
- Customer complaints
- Vendor complaints
- Unexplained increases in accounts receivable
- Lack of supporting documentation

These are only a handful of the red flags indicating fraud, theft, and abuse of resources. Unfortunately, the risks can be much more critical than employee fraud, theft, or other misconduct.

In the first few months of 2009, we witnessed an incredibly disturbing barrage of violence directly related or somehow linked to the workplace. Innocent men, women, and children, and the police officers trying to save them were ruthlessly gunned down in separate incidents. Why does the workplace figure so prominently into instances of outrageous violence? This should not come as a surprise when we consider the importance of our jobs in our daily lives. After all, one of the first social questions asked is, "What do you do?"

Look at Maslow's Hierarchy of Needs. Starting at the base of the pyramid are the physiological needs such as sleep, food, and water. Next is safety to include our body, family, resources, health, and employment. Following are love and belonging, esteem and self-actualization. How many of those hierarchical needs are filled, whether directly or indirectly, through our careers? Many of the workplace violence incidents involved a real or imagined threat to continued employment. A high unemployment rate, dwindling savings, and a sense of hopelessness create a volatile mixture.

By early 2009, I had given several presentations and interviews relative to the increasing risk of workplace violence and was receiving more requests for workplace violence training. How do we protect against potential workplace violence? By looking for the red flags. Here are a few of the warning signs as offered by the United States Office of Personnel Management:

- Direct or veiled threats of harm
- Intimidating, belligerent, harassing, bullying, or other inappropriate and aggressive behavior
- Numerous conflicts with supervisors and other employees
- Bringing a weapon to the workplace, brandishing a weapon in the workplace, making inappropriate references to guns, or fascination with weapons

- Statements showing fascination with incidents of workplace violence, statements indicating approval of the use of violence to resolve a problem, or statements indicating identification with perpetrators of workplace homicides
- Statements indicating desperation (over family, financial, and other personal problems) to the point of contemplating suicide
- Drug/alcohol abuse
- Extreme changes in behaviors

Again, these are just a few examples. Workplace violence is a risk that warrants on-site training.

The red lights of corporate excess were blinking when then Tyco CEO Dennis Kozlowski threw a multi-million dollar party for his wife, partially funded by Tyco and billed as a shareholder meeting. One of the most prominent displays of excess was the ice sculpture of the Statue of David with vodka spewing from…you know where. Did anybody take notice that a moral hazard was staring them in the face? Maybe not.

There is one very effective method for identifying red flags—listen. As simple as that sounds, it is often overlooked, especially by management. Bosses like to be in charge and show that they have the right ideas. That is why they became bosses. While as a boss, you should be able to add value to the work of your subordinates by giving them guidance, your subordinates are probably closer to any problem brewing in the workplace. They will notice changes in personal and professional conduct, violations of rules and procedures, and many of the other red flags and may be in a position to provide you with valuable guidance; assure communications are flowing in both directions.

There may be a natural aversion to "snitching" on a fellow employee or superior. Whether it is a personal matter or fear of reprisal, that reluctance exists. Your subordinates will probably drop hints as to what concerns them. Listen to them and you will hear the questions that they are hoping you ask. They want to be able to tell themselves that you figured it out or you "got it out" of them.

How often do we wonder, "Why didn't I see that coming?" Usually there were warning signs, but they were much more obvious in hindsight. We all get absorbed in the demands of the moment, of continuous raging fires that need to get extinguished. There seems to be little time to watch for these warning signs. We can more effectively see these red flags by understanding them and encouraging all our employees to take ownership in the process. After all...

CHAPTER 6

Lesson: It's All About the Team
Or, "Hey, how are *we* going to get this bastard in jail?"

Remember what we discussed earlier about numbers. We like numbers—more, more, and more. More means better. As a police officer and as an FBI agent, my performance was measured in numbers—how many tickets; how many arrests, indictments, and convictions; how much economic loss prevented; how many violent acts prevented; and so on. When you are measured by numbers, you try to keep those numbers high. We know that when assessing performance, you get what you measure. There was one basic truth about a statistical accomplishment. There were no fractions and no way to share the credit for a singular arrest or other statistical accomplishment. If you were fortunate to have several arrests out of a case, you could divvy them up, but rarely was there enough to go around to everyone's satisfaction. As a cop, most of what you accomplished—your tickets and arrests—was done individually and was yours to claim. Though there were times when things were not that clear.

Each investigation in the FBI was assigned to a case agent. Sometimes there was a co-case agent or a task force officer from another agency who worked as a partner on the case. There were big cases and little cases; important cases and not-so-important cases; cases that would get you recognition and cases that would leave you in the dark. Make no mistake, the FBI had no shortage of big egos. We all wanted the big cases. Everyone wanted the "face time." A big case got them time with the top brass; everyone wanted to see their name in the newspaper or their face on television; and everyone dreamed of writing a book. Accordingly, it was important that the supervisors assigned cases fairly, so that every agent had a shot at a big case. In my experience, that did not seem to happen. Once a supervisor found a favorite agent or two, those favorites seemed to prosper at the professional expense of the other agents. I recall the bitterness and hostility that developed when the team concept was so blatantly ignored, and I also remember how well the cases were investigated on the occasions when the supervisor promoted teamwork and fairness.

On my drug squad in New York, there was an agent I will call Arnie. Arnie was a solid agent. As a former Marine, he focused on the mission with incredible intensity. You could see the look in his eye; he was going to take that hill. Arnie just naturally became an informal leader on the squad; he was seen as a model agent, someone "who really had his shit together." I must admit to being somewhat envious of his reputation and the respect he commanded.

One night, I was just sitting in the office and heard Arnie and another agent I'll refer to as Dave, call in on the radio that they were attempting a fugitive arrest and gave the address. Dave was a different kind of agent. He always tagged along with Arnie. It was a little funny and a little pitiful at the same time. I was not sure why two agents were out on a fugitive arrest by themselves. There were several of us in the office. I knew by the address that they were close by. A little voice in my head told me to go help. I got up and went.

As I pulled onto the block, I saw Arnie and Dave approach a vehicle. Unfortunately, they did not completely block in the subject's vehicle. He stepped on the gas, drove over snow banks, and was off. I could not believe what I was seeing. I had not had a vehicle pursuit in more than ten years, since I was a cop. Nervously, I fumbled for my red light and siren switch. I called in the pursuit on the radio, and the race was on. Snow covered the street signs and the streets. It was dark, and after pursuing him deep into the neighborhood, I had no idea of where I was. Arnie and Dave apparently did not get back in their car fast enough to catch up with us. I was alone.

Eventually, I turned a corner onto a long block that had no intersections; it just let back out onto the same street about a half mile down. I started to pursue, then realized that his car could not have gotten off the street that fast. I slowed down and started looking around a little more carefully. I found his car parked off to the side of the street. Then, I saw fresh footprints leading towards a house and I spotted him. He was at the back corner of the house getting ready to run into the backyard. Do not ask me how, but I somehow convinced him that I would shoot him if he did not stop. He gave up. He was a suspect in a homicide. He was twenty-five years old, and as I handcuffed him and patted him down, it was obvious that he was a bodybuilder. Put all those factors together, and I was glad I did not have to chase him and potentially fight him. He probably could have and would have killed me—not figuratively, but literally. That was the catalyst for me to start thinking about getting off the street and into management.

We were not accustomed to, nor were we very experienced in, vehicle pursuits in the FBI. I could not get on the radio, with everybody calling in trying to find my location. Unlike the police department, the FBI did not understand and practice strict radio discipline. Not that I did not appreciate the concern, but the lack of radio discipline and protocol proved dangerous. Remember, I did not have a cell phone back then. Realizing that I was not going to get a chance to radio in my position, I just sat on my prisoner until a neighbor came out and asked how he could help. He called the FBI office, and within minutes, help arrived.

When Dave came on the scene, he grabbed my arrestee, now handcuffed by me, and started getting in his face, talking real tough to him. That was kind of humorous. It was easy to act tough after the fact and while the suspect was handcuffed behind his back. Dave and Arnie took the prisoner back to the office for processing. As soon as we got back, agents who were not on the scene went up to

Arnie to congratulate him on the arrest. "Don't congratulate me; Tabman caught him," were the first words out of Arnie's mouth. Arnie did the right thing; he gave me my fifteen minutes of fame. I also felt good knowing that even Arnie made mistakes and I was able to help out. It gave me a renewed feeling about being part of a team.

In the FBI, I had a reputation for being a bit of a lone wolf; I did not hang out much after work and usually had lunch just sitting at my desk by myself. While I was always willing to help on any investigation, I think some of the cops and agents were hesitant to ask me; my loner tendencies did not exude a welcoming atmosphere. That was not intentional, but I did not do anything to change that. After that arrest, I realized that I needed to be more proactive in letting the squad know that I wanted to be a part of the team. Slowly, I did become more a part of the squad by offering to help and not waiting to be asked; I enjoyed it. A few months later, I was assigned a major drug and money laundering investigation that took over one year to resolve. We conducted long surveillances, wiretaps, hidden cameras; it was a lot of work, but a lot of fun too. The team was there for me every step of the way, and we were successful. Arrests were made worldwide. Millions of dollars were seized. The main subject is, or should be, still sitting in prison having received a sentence of 660 years.

Let's go back to my old partner Carl. One afternoon, he got on the radio in an incredibly calm voice to tell the dispatcher that he was in a high-speed pursuit of a motorcycle. Those were tough pursuits. Motorcycles were able to go down alleys through which our cars could not follow. The motorcycle was heading south on a local street. I was able to head north on that same street within a few seconds. I saw the motorcycle coming with Carl's flashing red lights right behind him. I was not sure of what to do. There was no realistic way to block his passage and I could not place my car in the path of Carl's fast approaching car. My plan was to try to open my door into the fleeing motorcyclist as he passed to knock him down. When he saw me, he tried to make a sharp turn and tumbled off his bike. The foot pursuit was on.

Fresh out of the academy, I was in good shape but soon realized how hard it was to run in full uniform, with a heavy belt of equipment and a bulletproof vest. Carl was a marathon runner, and I expected him to pass me shortly, but he didn't. His dangling equipment got caught up on the fence he tried to jump. I finally trapped the fleeing scoundrel and wrestled him to the ground. In control and handcuffing him, I saw Carl coming around the corner. He jumped into the air, screeched a karate-type yell, landed on the prisoner, picked him up by his neck, pinned him against the fence, and told him, "That will teach you to run from the police."

Off Carl went with his arrest. It was his call and his arrest. My job, as a team member, was to help every other team member the best I could, with or without statistical credit. The next day at roll call, Carl complimented me in front of the squad and our sergeant—our team. That kind of recognition, though informal and fleeting, was the best type of credit a rookie cop could ask for.

On another shift, Carl committed an even greater act of teamwork. One day, he was called to a residential burglary. Burglaries were routine, mundane calls. You took some notes, dusted for fingerprints, knocked on a few neighbors' doors looking for potential witnesses, and wrote up a report for detectives to follow up on. Carl got on the radio and asked that I respond to the scene of the burglary. I was not sure what he wanted, but I got there quickly. Carl asked if I wanted to take this call. Not that I wouldn't take a call for him, but it was unusual for him to ask. Naturally, I asked why. Carl, a happily married guy, looked at me with a smile and said, "Look over there; she's the complainant." I looked, and I liked what I saw. She was quite an attractive young woman. I willingly agreed to take the call. After all, it's all about teamwork, right? I investigated this burglary slowly and methodically. What came out of that call? We wound up dating for quite a while. I guess I considered that as Carl's little way of making up for me catching his fleeing motorcyclist. That was more than twenty years ago. I still remember that true display of teamwork.

A friend of mine worked for a well-known beverage company. One day he gave me a sample of a new drink soon being unveiled. I took one sip and could not believe what I had just tasted. I tried to hide my expression, but it had the most disgusting taste of any soft drink I had ever had. At first, I thought it was a joke. It was no joke. At least not until it was introduced onto the market. It flopped terribly. At a later date, over dinner, I asked my friend if the company looked closely at who was responsible for bringing this failure to market. Would the company punish the person(s) responsible for such a disaster? "Of course not," he replied, surprised that I even asked that question. He explained that such a move would stifle creativity. Besides, no one person was responsible for this; it was a corporate (i.e., team) failure. Learn and move on. This made so much sense that I started to wonder why I even asked that question. Then I realized the unfortunate truth.

That question was based on my own experiences. The FBI was nothing like this corporation. As soon as something went bad, there was a lot of blaming and ass covering in the FBI. There was no "we," no collective responsibility. At the first sign of trouble, the FBI pointed a finger, blamed, accused, and then punished. The truth was figured out somewhere down the line, maybe. Unless, the responsible party was a member of that inner circle; then, somehow, the wagons were circled. The FBI has a lot to learn from this beverage company.

So how do you build that team concept in your business? There will always be competition amongst the team members. For bonuses, promotions, or just big egos, members of your team will want to outdo their coworker. A certain amount of competition can serve as a motivator. I do not believe retreats into the woods or falling backwards into a group or playing silly games builds camaraderie or a sense of team. Maybe the boss hosting a family barbeque could help add a little of the personal touch needed for a close team, but only to a limited degree. Most importantly, everyone needs a chance to shine, to get their fifteen minutes of fame. If they are not succeeding in one position, they may in another. Everyone wants to feel that he is contributing to the team's success.

For example, one of my senior agents was just not performing up to expectations. He was seeking a transfer to another division via a promotion to supervisor. In the FBI, many managers were often quick to move problems elsewhere rather than address them. They would recommend someone for a promotion though the person clearly did not deserve it, just to avoid confrontation. I was not going to do that, and I told the employee so. Performance would have to improve before I would sign off on any request for a promotion or transfer. A few months later, I started an initiative that required a significant amount of effort in non-traditional investigative duties. I offered it to this agent. He accepted and in a short time, I saw a reinvigorated agent whose performance was improving and rising to management's level of expectations. By getting that recognition, he was becoming more a part of the team, interacted more with his coworkers, and was more willing to voluntarily help other agents with their work. Sometimes it takes a little effort and time to find a place in the organization where a person can become most effective.

Ensure that everyone gets the assistance they need from their coworkers and rewards are shared fairly. Nobody wants to see his contribution go unrecognized. As a boss, you should not be everyone's friend; that is not the key to building a team. Their mutual respect for you as a leader, not as a friend, is what will bind them as a team. I was always concerned with managers who were extremely well liked by everyone; what that indicated to me was that they were not making the tough calls. Give the team a vision and a road map for achieving its goals and let them go out and accomplish that together. Recognize their collective efforts to give them the team identity and the desire to work cooperatively. Treat your people with respect and dignity; encourage everyone to, as the song says, "give a little more than you're asking for," and the team will build on its own.

You must also be aware that there are certain personalities that have the potential to destroy a team. I believe they are the malcontents, rumor spreaders, gossipers, and whiners. These traits are related, and many times someone, unfortunately, possesses more than one of these traits. I remember once reading an article that claimed that "water cooler gossiping" had some value to the office. Maybe. I find these tendencies very destructive to the team. Malcontents try to bring everybody down; after all, misery loves company. The rumor spreaders can only be out to hurt other people; there is nothing to be gained by that. The gossipers, who may not be as deliberate and as vindictive as the rumor spreaders, transmit information that usually has no basis of fact and is usually just as harmful. The whiner becomes someone nobody wants to work with, destroying the fiber of the team. You will want to work with and coach these people and hopefully bring them around. If they do not improve, have a plan and policies for dealing with them. Can you transfer them to another assignment where they will not be able to spread their ill will so easily? Do not let them bring the entire team down.

The teamwork of Continental Airlines during the massive blackout of August 14, 2003, was highlighted in Rosabeth Moss Kanter's book *Confidence*. While most of the airports and airlines were in chaos, Continental canceled only a fraction of the number of flights canceled by its major competitors. Kanter points out, "For the two days after the blackout, Continental's gross revenues were $4.34 million above normal forecasts." She attributes Continental's success to their working, instinctively, as a team who "… trusted one another to do the right thing."

This concept of trusting one another as an important component of a successful team is mentioned in the book *The Five Dysfunctions of a Team*. Author Patrick M. Lencioni cites lack of trust as one of the major dysfunctions. Just to complete that thought, the other four dysfunctions that Lencioni identifies are: 1) fear of conflict: this is the inability of teams to engage in "passionate debate of ideas"; 2) lack of commitment, which is almost self-explanatory— everybody must be committed to the same goals; 3) avoidance of accountability; and 4) inattention to results, which "occurs when team members put their individual needs (such as ego, career development, or recognition) or even the needs of their divisions above the collective goals of the team."

In the book *Teams That Click*, by the Harvard Business School Press, one of the chapters is entitled "The Three Essentials of an Effective Team," by Jim Billington. The three essentials that Billington cites are commitment, competence, and a common goal. You can see that certain themes repeat themselves in the various theories of successful teams.

A police squad is a unique example of a team. Each officer is out there on his own. Yet, at any given moment, he is dependent upon any one of his team members. One of the greatest feelings of teamwork I experienced was when I was a young patrol officer.

One night on patrol, I noticed two suspicious young men meandering around a shopping plaza. Signaling for them to stay where they were as I approached to question them, I was a little surprised they did not run as soon as they saw me. As was routine protocol, I called it in on the radio, and my partner, Carl, was notified so that he would start that way for backup, just in case. Carl replied to the dispatcher that he was at the opposite end of the sector and it would be a few minutes before he could get over there. The dispatcher acknowledged that, and at that moment, there was no immediate concern. As I started talking to these two, it became apparent that they were up to something. Maybe they were planning on burglarizing a store or breaking into a car, but they were not just innocently hanging out. I did not know exactly what they were up to, but something criminal was afoot.

As I kept speaking with them, they started to become a little bolder and more aggressive with me. When I noticed that they were moving in a circular pattern, trying to get one of them behind me, I knew I was in trouble. At that moment, the dispatcher called to check on me. With one hand on my weapon, I did not want to tug at the radio on my belt. I knew that if I did not answer the dispatcher, that would trigger an emergency response from other units. Carl was not very close. The next closest unit was out of his car on a call. Not sure how fast backup would make it, I started playing the shuffle and dance routine, trying to keep them from closing in on me.

Concerned that time was running out on me, I became nervous, thinking that a two-on-one wrestling match was imminent. Somehow, within seconds I heard Carl's sirens. Then I saw the flashing lights of another officer speeding to the scene from the opposite direction. The two officers came barreling over the hills and converged on us simultaneously, flying out of their cars, batons in hand. Each officer grabbed one of the guys, applied a little baton-meets-ass action, and had them down in seconds. Without lifting a finger, I was safe.

When in danger, the moments generally feel like hours. Yet, I remember only how fast my backup came. The intensity of their response when I was in danger, the look on their faces, and their obvious commitment to my safety are burned into my memory. Not that I needed to be any more inspired about being part of that team, but even as I write about this, more than twenty-five years later, I relive that feeling of brotherhood that overcame me that night; it was overwhelming. Those experiences may explain why Carl and I, two very different personalities, who have lived far from each other over the years, are still friends.

This event was more than just a cop story. Surprisingly, it reflected an extremely efficient business process. First, the dispatcher and I followed established procedure by properly utilizing the radio. Through effective and efficient communications, the police jargon relayed a tremendous amount of information very quickly with very few words. That was important to get quick responses and to leave the radio open for me, in case I did need to call in again. By not taking action (not answering the radio), I was confident that a certain series of events would follow, which they did. Think about it—by not taking action, the process worked flawlessly. That should be a goal of all your business processes.

So, getting back to the team concept—we want a close, cohesive team. Can there a downside to that? There are potential dangers in team dynamics. One specific danger you should be alert for is the phenomenon known as groupthink. This term was coined by William H. White in 1952. Wikipedia defines groupthink as "a decision making process, where the group members go along with what they believe is the consensus. Groupthink may cause groups to make hasty, irrational decisions, where individual doubts are set aside, for fear of upsetting the group's balance."

One of the most famous incidents often cited when discussing groupthink was the disastrous Bay of Pigs invasion. President Kennedy ordered this invasion, and apparently, his most trusted advisers did not warn him of its dangers and its unlikely success. Other major disasters have been deemed the result of groupthink. Do you see this in your business meetings, the concept of team taken to a dangerous extreme? Is individual thought stifled? Are good ideas or potential risks not being identified?

Groupthink was widespread in the FBI. Dissention did not get you invited into that inner circle; supporting the general consensus was an easier route. During my years in the FBI, watching who was being chosen for the top-level decision-making positions, I noticed that it was always from within that same inner circle. Promotions were highly predictable. During my twenty-three plus years, watching these agents, whom I knew from their earlier years, change as they began to conform to the inner circle model was almost distressing. There was, in the FBI, a "Stepford" quality to the top management team. The FBI's promotional process, despite the gift-wrapping, relied primarily on personal choices. Whom do people choose for their subordinates? They choose people they know, people they like and are comfortable with, and most important and most dangerous, people who think the same way they do. The result is a lack of intellectual diversity.

Irving Janus identified eight symptoms of groupthink:
1. A feeling of invulnerability, creating excessive optimism and encouraging risk taking.
2. Discounting warnings that might challenge assumptions.
3. An unquestioned belief in the group's morality, causing members to ignore the consequences of their actions.
4. Stereotyped views of enemy leaders.
5. Pressure to conform against members of the group who disagree.
6. Shutting down of ideas that deviate from the apparent group consensus.
7. An illusion of unanimity with regards to going along with the group.
8. Mindguards—self-appointed members who shield the group from dissenting opinions.

I wonder if these symptoms, especially number four, translate into misuses of the PATRIOT Act powers in our fight against terrorism. Agents appeared to categorize the acts of Muslims as terrorism where I do not believe they would have for another religion or ethnicity. Finding this common enemy served as a bonding tool for the agents.

There is an odd proverb I once heard and liked. It said that if you have one cow and you have one pig, you really have three animals. You have the cow; you have the pig; and you have the cow and the pig. The translation is somewhat obvious—the presence of another being changes our behavior. I remember this vividly during one of my assignments in headquarters.

I was friendly with two agents we'll call Joe and Al. Joe and Al were close friends and generally stuck together. I would enjoy discussing politics and world affairs with Joe. With Al, I enjoyed playing racquetball and talking about women. Separately, I liked each one. One day, the three of us were sitting together in my office just talking about nothing in particular, and I couldn't resist saying something that I absolutely felt. I first turned to Joe and said, "I like you," and then looking at Al said, "And I like you." Then I looked at them both, pointing to first one and then the other, and said, "But I don't like you and you." Though a bit arrogant, it was the truth. I found that when they were together they fed off each other and took on new personas with whom I did not like socializing. I was seeing the cow and the pig as one animal.

Shortly before this book went to publication, I read on on-line article from msnbc.com, entitled, *Smile! It might just help the economy*. In this article, author Dan Pashman points out how contagious human emotions can be. While the article focuses on the economic climate, the application of this theory is relevant to other business environments. Pashman quotes Wharton professor Sigal Barsade,

" 'People are mood inductors...We're social beings, we influence each other...We most often don't realize it's happening. People are very unaware of where their moods come from.' " Pashman also cites a very telling study, "... team leaders were shown different videos designed to put them in certain moods, then told to lead groups in tasks. The group members ended up in the same moods as the videos that their respective leaders watched, even though the group members themselves never even watched the videos.

I have witnessed the danger of this phenomenon several times during my FBI career. When FBI executive management wished to "take someone out" (i.e. ruin a career), there was no better opportunity than during the inspection of the field office. The directions that were given and the tone in which they were communicated set the environment for the inspection team, as well as signaling management's expectations. The conduct of the inspection team, how questions were asked, and how information was spun, led to the pre-determined conclusion. The inspection team leadership was capable of setting a "blood in the water" environment and the subordinate team began circling like sharks. This was partly due to the "mob mentality" and partly due to the realization that failure to fall in line while conducting an inspection could prove to be professional suicide in the FBI. However, it was disturbing to see the behavior and mindset of FBI agents so easily manipulated.

The lack of independent thought as the mob mentality descends upon a group is addressed by Eric Hoffer in his thought–provoking book, *The True Believer*. Hoffer points out that "action" is a group unifier. He states, "Men of thought seldom work well together, whereas between men of action there is usually an easy camaraderie. Teamwork is rare in intellectual or artistic undertakings, but common and almost indispensible among men of action." Remember this as you promote teamwork in your organization. If someone does not perform well within the teamwork concept, there may be a very good reason.

Also, do not go to Abilene. What does that mean? The Abilene Paradox was developed in 1974 by Professor Jerry Harvey of George Washington University, having originated from a real-life story. The parable of the Abilene Paradox is about four adults who were sitting around, apparently bored, in 100+ degree weather in a small town outside of Abilene, Texas. One of them suggested that they drive to a certain cafeteria in Abilene, for no particular reason, and they did so in a car without air conditioning. The meal was nothing special, and everybody was generally unhappy with the trip. After returning home, they all discovered that not one of them thought the trip was a good idea but went along, thinking the others were eager to go. Had one spoken up or even questioned the value of the trip, they would have probably spared themselves a miserable day. This is not an uncommon group characteristic, and it is counter-productive.

A close cohesive team is important for success. However, there are undesirable team dynamics for which you must be alert, or the team will not function optimally.

There are several ways to avoid groupthink. Honestly encourage dissent. Seek intellectual diversity. Diversity does not come naturally to us. That is why organizations have diversity programs to counteract the natural phenomenon of choosing people "like ourselves." Use consultants for a disinterested third-party opinion when appropriate. Brainstorm and thoroughly discuss ideas. A group decision that appears in any way to have been derived by groupthink should get a thorough risk assessment. Can you think of other administrations since JFK who appeared to be subject to groupthink?

While I have absolutely no knowledge nor insight as to how the Iraq weapons of mass destruction issue evolved, after all these years in the FBI, I am going to guess. I imagine that the informal word going around the CIA was to the effect: "Do you want to be the analyst to tell the president that he cannot go to war?"

On the one hand, being a cooperative member of a team is important. On the other hand, when your decisions do not turn out as planned, don't look for the team behind you; you better be prepared to go it alone. A retired New York City Police commander gave me some advice before I embarked on my police career. He said, "Young man, just remember this, nobody cares about you except your mother." Those are words I have lived by. Within the concept of teamwork lies another concept, one of...

CHAPTER 7

Lesson: <u>Partnership</u>
Or, "OK, let's stop competing; we'll do it together."

Let's distinguish a partnership as a smaller, more personal joint effort rather than being a member of a bigger corporate team. As a police officer, Carl was my partner, but the rest of the squad and the police department was my team. I was no less responsive to anyone on the squad than I was to Carl, but a personal bond developed simply by the constant act of helping and at times saving each other. Partnerships, while sometimes forced upon us, are usually chosen for personal or professional benefit. A primary example is choosing a life partner and deciding to marry.

A team cannot and will not function effectively if the team members do not see the corporate enterprise as their partner. Maybe not a partner as direct and dependable as Carl was to me, but a partner in achieving the corporate goal. For example, a sales representative may work on his own all day, with little or no interaction with the company. That separation must be addressed to avoid a feeling of isolation, lack of direction and corporate indifference to the employee's success and well-being. Here, communications become vital. Occasional telephone calls, a video conference and emails to keep the employee up-to-date, will fill that void and keep the employee engaged. If he is going to be successful and emanate enthusiasm and a belief in the product, he must feel connected to the company, having some sense of a partnership with the corporate team. In view of the growing popularity of telecommuting, corporations should be aware that physical distance and lack of personal interaction can nullify any feelings of a partnership. To develop a sense of partnership with their employees, corporations should use fair compensation, reasonable benefits, flexibility, and other morale-building accommodations.

Formal partnerships usually form by necessity. Informal partnerships are usually formed by choice as people take a liking to one another and just tend to work together. Sometimes these informal groups are called cliques.

Cliques are formed in all social arenas: work, school, neighborhoods, and even places of worship. Clique is a term usually used with pejorative intent. That is not appropriate. Cliques are a natural social phenomenon. Small groups will always form from larger ones. There is just a natural tendency to stay close to people we find that we can bond with. Personality, similar beliefs, common interests, hobbies, or any number of things draw people together.

One of my longtime friends from the FBI is Jerry. Jerry and I come from very different backgrounds and did not work together until the twilight years of our careers when we were assigned to headquarters together. So how did we become such good friends?

As you progress in management in the FBI, there is much travel. You must go on several inspections and attend numerous meetings and conferences held at different locations. During these times, if invited to join a group for a meal, I would usually accept; yet I would not seek groups out, satisfied to be alone. Most people would go out to lunch or dinner in big groups; I preferred small groups. Some would go out drinking later on, which was not something I was inclined to do. After being with the same people all day for a number of days, I usually found myself wanting a little solitude. Often I would find a quiet place to eat and then head out to some place such as a bookstore to browse or to the gym for a late workout. In doing so, I would many times run into Jerry, who would also be on his own. He too did not like being with a crowd. We both liked computers, and though we had different political ideals, we enjoyed discussing politics. So, what made us friends were not only the things we liked but the things we both did not like. Friends are partners; you are working together for a common goal, which is primarily someone to share social activities with, share secrets with, or rely on when you are in need.

There was a story in the FBI that I have heard since I was in the academy. I heard it so often that I do believe it is more urban legend than fact. The story goes that the FBI had an agent who infiltrated the mob. He was living alone in an undercover apartment with an undercover identity. Once, very late at night, the agent got sick and called his "handling agent," or basically, his partner, to get him to the hospital. Given the time of night, his partner declined to come get him. Left with few options, the undercover agent called one of his mob "partners" he developed while working undercover. The mobster immediately hung up the phone, rushed over to the agent's apartment, and took him to the hospital. Whether this story is true or not true does not really matter; the point was to drive home the importance of what defines a true partnership.

I observed a remarkable display of partnership once when I was back at the FBI Academy for some in-service. I was in the gym locker room after a workout, and a class of recruits was returning from their physical fitness test. This was a very important test. A recruit would not graduate from the academy and become an FBI Special Agent unless they passed all aspects of the test, and there were several, including a two-mile run. One recruit walked in to the locker room, quite despondent, as he had not finished the run within the required time. He told the young man sitting next to me on the bench that he had to go out and run it again. The young man responded, "I'll go out and run it with you." I was incredibly impressed by that sense of camaraderie. I turned to him and said, with a poor attempt at humor, "That's pretty decent of you. I wouldn't run that thing twice for my mother." He then turned to me and said, "Yeah, well sometimes roommates are more important than mothers." I was in awe of what I thought was a brilliant statement and generally a great comeback. If I knew this agent's name, I would give him credit, because he could not have been any more correct. A true partner can be one of the most valuable assets in life.

Law enforcement agencies have taken on more and more partnerships to address the growing sophistication of crime. The big partnerships the FBI touts are the Joint Terrorism Task Forces in every FBI field office. Federal, state, and local law enforcement agencies participate on these task forces, and all bring something of value to the table. Illegal immigration is clearly a problem related to terrorism. The Immigration and Customs Enforcement (ICE) agency is of great importance. Drugs are trafficked and street crimes are committed to raise money in support of terrorism. Accordingly, the Drug Enforcement Administration (DEA) and the local police are important partners as are numerous other agencies. These partnerships must work to serve the American people, however, they do not exist without conflicts and differences of opinion; but their vital existence demands that these agencies overcome such hurdles. One motivating factor of cooperation is the reality that no agency wants to be viewed as a nonparticipant in the war on terror.

The FBI does form partnerships with the local law enforcement community on other crime problems, despite old stories of the FBI snubbing local police. In my management positions, I worked closely with the local police chiefs and sheriffs and formed some good friendships, even though we were usually of much different backgrounds and personality types. The relationships extended beyond work, and many of these chiefs and sheriffs have been to my family functions. Close friendships on the personal level will help partnerships on the corporate level. Such friendships cannot be forced; they must develop naturally.

One of the best interagency partnerships I had in the FBI was when we formed a joint Cyber Crime Task Force with the Secret Service. We shared jurisdiction over a number of crimes committed in cyber land, especially identity theft. At the headquarters level in D.C., the two agencies were quite the rivals, each courting Congress for more money and primary jurisdiction. On the local level, I worked with my counterpart at the Secret Service, Kurt. The task force facilities were funded by the FBI, and the FBI had twice the number of people assigned to the task force. The agreement was an equal partnership; we shared equal authority and responsibility. If I had been a consultant with that scenario proposed to me, I would not have recommended such a setup. Knowing the historic turf battles between law enforcement agencies and the general rule of one person in charge, I would have predicated failure. I would have been wrong.

At the time of my retirement, the task force was working successfully. There was one very good reason, and that was my partner, Kurt. He did not have the traditional big law enforcement ego; he was honest, sincere, and always credited the FBI if he was speaking publicly about cyber crime. His demeanor and personality let me, if not forced me, to bring my defenses down. As friends, we would not let a difference of opinion ruin the great partnership. Our subordinates, aware of our friendship, knew that it was best to resolve any differences on their level. We joked that we could not let our respective headquarters know how well we were getting along.

Partnerships, however, can be uneasy and filled with pitfalls, especially the ones that are forced upon you. When I was working drug cases back in New York City during the 1980s and 1990s, the FBI was forced to partner up with the DEA on most cases. This was not because we really wanted to, but because it seemed that we were always targeting the same subject. The partnership always started nicely with pledges of cooperation and information sharing. I cannot remember one that ended that way. One agency always saw themselves as getting screwed by the other agency, and the investigations usually ended prematurely out of an inability to develop a mutually agreed upon long-term strategy. I am not faulting either agency, but those partnerships "in appearance only" did not protect our citizens.

Good partnerships must be viewed as good neighbors—you need good fences. Everyone should have a clear, documented description of each partner's respective role, duties, and responsibilities. There must be some forum for resolving issues rather than arguing and rushing to the finish line before the goal is met. Just as ineffective is having to reach one of those compromises that we discussed earlier that do not really work best but allow everyone to save face. Partnerships can be great but are fraught with peril.

I know of very few friends who have partnered up in small businesses or professional practices wherein both the business and the friendship survived.

There is another phenomenon that intrigues me when it comes to partners. That is game theory, which was founded by a mathematician named John Von Neumann. Game theory is a study of human behavior that incorporates math, economics, and a variety of behavioral sciences. Its studies give fascinating insight into human nature and motivation. One of the more popular "games" under the rubric of game theory is the Prisoners' Dilemma developed by A. W. Tucker, a highly accomplished mathematician and game theorist. Appropriately, for this book, it discusses two partners, partners in crime.

Two men, Rob and Scott, are found by the police near the scene of a burglary. The police question them, pat them down, and arrest them for carrying concealed weapons. The burglary cannot be proven at the moment. The police take them into custody and question them separately. Here are the options each man must confront. If one confesses and implicates the other in the burglary, the one who confesses goes free and the other gets twenty years in prison. If both confess, then neither one's testimony is necessary and no deal to go free is offered to either one of them. For confessing, they will each get sentenced to ten years instead of the potential twenty. That, however, is only if they both confess. If neither confesses, there is insufficient evidence to prove the burglary, and each one will be sentenced to only one year for the concealed weapon. Neither Rob nor Scott knows what the other one plans on doing. The payoff chart looks like this:

	Scott confesses	Scott does not confess
Rob confesses	Both get ten years	Rob 0, Scott gets 20 years
Rob does not confess	Rob gets 20 years, Scott 0	Both get one year

As partners, the best plan is for neither of them to confess, each assuring that he and his partner get the minimum sentence without hurting the other. Is that what will happen? Probably not. Individually, each will worry that his partner may confess and implicate him, resulting in a twenty-year sentence while his partner goes free. It is more likely that each will confess, resulting in ten-year sentences. This is the reality of partnerships; we still look out for ourselves first. How confident would you be with your partner?

Businesses use partnerships all the time, to accomplish their goals. A good friend of mine started a successful chain of clothing stores. He eventually sold out to a larger company. He did not like the deal he got, but he wanted to sell and that was the best deal he could find. He recently started a new line of specialty clothing stores. For some reason, despite his previous successes, he could not get adequate financing. That same company he sold to earlier, offered to finance him, making themselves the partner with the majority interest in the business. He did not like the deal he was being offered. He did not like their style of doing business. He did not want to partner with them. Most importantly, he did not believe that he had any other realistic options. Finally, he did partner with them. He still does not like the deal, their company, or the way they do business, but he knew what he was getting into. He knew the ground rules. Now, with his stores extremely successful, he has no regrets.

Partnerships turn into teams. Mergers and acquisitions (M&As) occur as two entities "partner up" to capitalize on each other's strengths. They must learn each other's culture and business practices and eventually blend into a team. How well does that work? Ask AOL and Time Warner or Exxon and Mobil; you will probably get two different answers. No, these are not perfect examples; the situation and nature of the businesses affect the results. In researching M&As, I found one recurring theme when the merger/acquisition was considered a failure in terms of growth, improving the company's competitive edge, or increasing shareholder value; that was the failure to properly integrate corporate cultures. Corporate cultures are intangible and immeasurable, and therefore, the results of trying to merge them cannot be predicted with any degree of certainty. Numerous sources of information cited a study by KPMG regarding M&As. KPMG found that 83 percent of M&As did not produce any business benefit for the shareholder, and in fact, more than one-half of the M&As had a deleterious effect on value.

One notorious example of a merger within the federal government was the formation of the Department of Homeland Security. This department merged twenty-two government agencies with over 170,000 employees having disparate functions, policies, methods, and goals and objectives. In this merger, however, each agency did not lose its individual identity and become absorbed into one entity. For example, the Secret Service was moved from under the Treasury Department to Homeland Security. Their responsibilities for presidential and other VIP protection and certain financial crimes did not change. As a matter of fact, per the PATRIOT Act, their responsibilities in electronic crimes were somewhat expanded.

While there were numerous responsibilities to be assumed by the new Department of Homeland Security, clearly the 9/11 terrorist attacks were the impetus behind its formation. Their primary goal was to detect and deter another terrorist attack. Interestingly, the two primary agencies for detecting and deterring terrorist attacks— the FBI, domestically, and the CIA, abroad—were specifically excluded from the Department of Homeland Security. Certainly, one would have to question whether the Department of Homeland Security could or should be considered a serious effort with a high likelihood of success when two lead agencies integral to achieving its primary objectives are not member agencies. Yes, there are established policies and procedures for coordination and sharing of information. If past performance is the best predictor of future performance, how well coordination and sharing of information will fare is questionable.

How successful has the Department of Homeland Security been? One could point out that we have not had another terrorist attack since 9/11, at the time of this writing. Can a cause-and-effect relationship be drawn between the formation of the department and the absence of a terrorist attack? I do not see one. In an online (usatoday.com) article in USA TODAY, entitled *Ex-official tells of Homeland Security failures*, author Mimi Hall lists a number of troubling findings by the Department of Homeland Security Inspector General. Two examples are:

- Undercover investigators snuck weapons and explosives past security screeners at 15 airports in 2003.
- Air Marshals slept on the job, tested positive for drugs or alcohol, lost their weapons and falsified information in 2002.

In July 2009, the General Accountability Office announced that undercover investigators were able to carry liquid explosives and detonators past Federal Protective Service officers, posted at federal buildings. The Federal Emergency Management Agency (FEMA), which also was subsumed by the Department of Homeland Security, has been criticized for its handling of the crises caused by hurricanes and floods.

During my tenure as an SAC with the FBI, I worked closely and directly with senior executives of agencies under the Department of Homeland Security. I never observed any value or benefit derived from the department's formation. When I would ask my counterparts within those agencies what the Department of Homeland Security did and how it added value to their agency or to the government's war on terror, they could not give an answer. This is somewhat analogous to the survey by KPMG. What business (this business being the war on terror) benefit was derived, and what was the value to the stakeholder (American people) of this merger? That leaves the question that I cannot answer, which is why do we have the Department of Homeland Security at all?

While the above examples address major corporate and government mergers, the message is that partnerships are difficult at any level. At the beginning of the chapter, we mentioned the most personal of all partnerships—marriage. What is the failure rate of those partnerships? A business partnership must have identifiable benefits and add value to each partner's bottom line. Otherwise, the pitfalls of partnerships will prevail and failure will follow.

Last on this subject is another aspect of partnerships, cliques, and social groupings that leads, at least indirectly, to an issue that has been haunting law enforcement for many years now. That is the issue of racial profiling. Racial profiling, whereby someone is targeted for investigation solely upon race, such as a Muslim being suspected of terrorism with no demonstrable connection to terrorism, is clearly wrong, bigoted, unethical, and illegal. As I have stated, there were occasions in my FBI career when I thought that was happening.

However, using ethnicity as one element of a profile is not wrong or immoral. A profile, as used in this context, is just a set of characteristics that may indicate involvement in crime or a criminal organization, which is a type of partnership. Race and ethnicity are characteristics of that profile. We discussed how people break down into smaller groups of people who are more like them; they form their own teams or partnerships. I challenge you to look at your own close circle of friends and families. I would bet that the overwhelming majority of those people share your race, religion, ethnicity, and general socioeconomic status.

We are an ethnically based society. That is not a prejudicial statement, just another social phenomenon. We tend to be drawn to our "own kind." Unfortunately, my first realization of that was at the cafeteria at the FBI Academy, when I was a new agent undergoing training. It was in 1983, and about two hundred new agents were going through their initial training at any one time. There were agents there from field offices on in-service training. There were police officers from all over the world there availing themselves of training opportunities. So, there were hundreds of people in the cafeteria at any one moment during mealtimes. I walked into the cafeteria with my tray of food and was immediately struck by the obvious racial divide reflected by where people sat. Predominantly, though not exclusively, African Americans were sitting together, Hispanics were sitting together, whites were with whites, and Asians with Asians. This was many years ago, and I have not been at the FBI Academy for a long time, nor do I expect to ever be back. Maybe it is different now, but back then, it could not have been any more obvious. Later in my career, when I would travel to largely attended meetings, conferences, or inspections, I would see the same phenomenon occur again. At restaurants, or even walking around a mall, when social groups would meet, the racial divide was so obvious that it was embarrassing, though never discussed. It was not a pleasant reality, but it was reality.

In July 2009, a police matter was highly publicized as an example of racial profiling. A police sergeant responded to a particular house, as a citizen called into the police a possible break-in by two men. What the concerned citizen actually observed was the homeowner, upon returning home, met by a jammed front door, which he tried to force open, giving the appearance of a forcible break-in. When the police sergeant arrived at the house, he encountered the homeowner, a respected Harvard professor, and asked the homeowner to show identification. Sometime after confirming that the professor was the homeowner, and this event was not a break-in, the homeowner was arrested for disorderly conduct. The homeowner was African-American; the police sergeant was white. Allegations of racial profiling abounded. News commentators cited statistics reflecting racial profiling, and self-proclaimed experts concluded this was racially motivated based on historical events. There was one problem—they were wrong. This was not an example of racial profiling.

The police sergeant was at the professor's home due to a call by a citizen. The sergeant did not single out the professor or suspect him of a crime based solely on his race. Upon their initial encounter, the sergeant did not become physically or verbally aggressive with the professor. The sergeant appears to have followed proper police procedure. The professor was not arrested for burglary, but for disorderly conduct. That arrest generated the accusations of racial profiling. Based on my experience, I know that it is possible that the professor, being confronted in his own home, may have become disorderly and challenged the sergeant in a way that left him no choice but to make the arrest. It is also possible that the police sergeant overreacted to the professor. We do not know what happened, or what words were exchanged between the sergeant and the professor. However, to jump to the conclusion that the arrest was racially motivated was rushing to judgment.

I have been in similar situations; sometimes they escalated beyond a level that appeared reasonable. The disorderly conduct charge against the professor was subsequently dropped. As a police officer, on occasion, I agreed to drop charges of assaulting a police officer and disorderly conduct; sometimes the arrest was necessary at the moment, but following through with prosecution did not seem appropriate. As a police recruit, I remember being cautioned that even a traffic ticket could escalate into a shooting through no fault of the police officer. I am not saying that cops are always right or that racial profiling does not exist. I am saying that the arrest of an African-American man by a white police officer, even in the events described above, does not automatically translate into racial profiling or prejudiced motivation.

When asked about the arrest of the Harvard professor, President Obama characterized the police as acting "stupidly." President Obama is a brilliant man and I expect him to be a great president. In this matter, he was wrong to weigh in. He did not have all the facts. His comments, as the president, only fueled the flames of hostility. Though he later acknowledged his poor choice of words, that was a blunder for our "Communicator in Chief." Let's not rush to judgment.

My company represented, as a non-attorney advocate, a retired federal employee who was suing a federal agency for disparate impact resulting from the agency's career development policies and procedures. In short, we contended that this government agency made noncompetitive selections in an arbitrary and capricious manner that resulted in disparate impact—basically, their method of noncompetitive selections tended to favor one particular gender/ethnicity to the unfair exclusion of others. When I deposed the head of this agency's Diversity Program, I asked why they even needed a Diversity Program. Wouldn't the federal government operate a career development program with absolute fairness and free of any discrimination? The program manager cited the phenomenon of selecting "people like us" when given the freedom to do so. "What policies or procedures do you have in place to protect against this phenomenon, especially in noncompetitive selections?" I asked. "None," was the response. That little statement said a lot.

The criminal element is no different than the rest of us. They are just people, albeit criminal in nature, who will surround themselves with their close circle of friends and family. When I was working against the mob in New York, yes, we were investigating almost exclusively males of Italian/Sicilian descent. The Mafia was an Italian/Sicilian organization. That does not translate into saying that all Italians and Sicilians were mobsters—not even close. When I was investigating Colombian cocaine trafficking, the targets of our investigations were young men and women of Colombian nationality. Why? Because the drug cartels were based in Colombia where the cocaine was cultivated, processed and then shipped to the United States. Once again, the Colombians relied upon their close circles of friends and family—people like themselves. Generally, they fell into certain age groups and engaged in certain behavior, like my drug-dealing friend Oscar. That was the profile. That is not the equivalent of saying all Colombians were drug dealers, which would be a foolish, bigoted, and just plain stupid thing to say. That is the same as with terrorism. Right now, Islamic extremism is the focal point of the terrorist threat against the United States. Without arguing the reasons why, that is the fact. So naturally, if we were to list the characteristics of the Islamic extremist terrorist, one would be an adherent of Islam. Once again, that does not translate into accusing all Muslims of being terrorists. There would be other characteristics such as probably male, certain age, and lifestyle. All those put together form the profile. The criminals and terrorists form their own profile, not law enforcement. Law enforcement only uses that profile as a tool.

How does profiling affect business? You probably do some form of profiling every day to protect your business and employees. Do you remember all those red flags we discussed earlier? Do you stay alert to patterns of conduct that you believe are indicators of potential workplace violence? When looking for and assessing those red flags, are you not forming a profile? When else may we form a profile? Think back to some of those other red flags. To protect your assets, do you remain aware of employees who attempt to gain access to places where they should not be, whether in the facility or computer databases? Are you alert to employees taking work or other items home when they shouldn't be? What about those employees who continuously come in early or work late, when no one else is around? Are they just dedicated employees, employees who need some quiet time to get their work done, or is there some more nefarious purpose? There are numerous indicators of employee theft that may be generic or specific to your company, some of which we discussed under Red Flags. When you take notice of behavior that may indicate crime or violence against your company, you are profiling, not by race but by actions and behavioral traits. Before you draw conclusions, you probably weigh other such factors as the employee's general conduct, nature of his conversations, social skills, background information, and work history. You are still looking at a set of criteria; you are forming a profile. Does phrasing this as "responding to red flag warnings" sound less prejudicial and controversial than profiling?

Partnerships have tremendous benefits. The offshoots of partnerships are cliques, social groupings and profiling which are fraught with risks. Following certain rules can help maximize the possibility of a successful partnership. Know yourself. Are you someone who enjoys working with a partner? Can you easily cooperate in decision making, share credit, jointly tackle problems, and equally accept blame? At school, my fourteen-year-old always asks permission to work alone when group projects are assigned. He knows that he wants to do it his way; he is not willing to risk a lower grade because of someone else's work and wants to work on his own schedule. We could extrapolate what that means for him in later life, but that is him and he knows himself. I am proud of that, especially because he inherited some of my lone wolf qualities. Know your partner, do your due diligence, and know what your partner would do in a prisoner's dilemma. In order to develop strong partnerships that can evolve into strong teams, you must...

CHAPTER 8

Lesson: <u>Be Kind to the Ego</u>
Or, "OK, we'll do it your way," when you really mean, "…until I figure out how to do it my way."

Very few, if any, of us operate in a vacuum. Our decisions, actions, and the things we say have reverberations up, down, and across the corporate environment. There are times when we know we are absolutely, positively right and the other person is wrong. Nobody likes being proven wrong. It hurts our ego. If you hurt someone's ego, your victory may prove short-lived.

In 1982, I was selected as the first full-time hostage negotiator on the Fairfax County Police Department SWAT team. Not that there had never been hostage negotiations before, but now the art and science of hostage negotiation were in vogue, popularized by the New York City Police Department, and the time had come to formalize that process.

My first negotiation occurred when I was a street cop, before I was promoted to the hostage negotiator position. A man in his early to mid thirties had taken his girlfriend hostage in the bathroom of the apartment they were sharing. I did not know if he was armed or if he had hurt her in any way. I began to speak to him through the locked door.

After a while, it became apparent that he really did not want anything other than for her to listen to him. I could not promise him that I would not arrest him, not knowing the whole situation. When he let her speak to me later during the negotiation, she sounded as if she had not been harmed. As time passed, it became apparent that the only thing he needed to end this was a way out that could save him some dignity. She agreed to sit down and talk, if he let her out. As they both asked me to stay for a while and speak with them, though she was clearly agreeing under duress, I concurred.

I did have backup waiting outside the door, but I did not want them in the apartment. I thought a show of force for a man who was already feeling belittled would only exacerbate the matter. Counseling was not really part of my job. I sacrificed twenty minutes and allowed him to save face in that he was able to look like he got what he wanted from his girlfriend and from the police. He was not armed; she had not been hurt; and she was very clear that she did not want to press charges. The crime had been committed in my presence, and I certainly could have arrested him irrespective of what she said. Domestic disputes account for a significant number of calls on patrol. A cop learns when it is and is not worth intervening. I took a little ribbing from the guys for being a "social worker" and not locking him up—and of course, forfeiting a good arrest stat. It turned out OK, and no one got hurt. Surprisingly, I never got called back there. What was the bottom line? The situation was defused simply by allowing this man to save face and not have his ego destroyed.

Another negotiation I conducted was after I was promoted to hostage negotiator. President Reagan had closed down the Libyan Embassy. It was a long time ago, and the politics of that are not important now. A Libyan government office in McLean, a wealthy town in Fairfax County, right outside Washington D.C., had come to be referred to as the Libyan Embassy. One morning, after a long night of surveillance, we got the call: "Takeover of the Libyan Embassy." This was clearly a SWAT operation. The subjects were Libyan nationals who were actually anti-Qaddafi and demanding more action from the United States government against the Qaddafi regime. We did not believe they had firearms, but you can never make that assumption. The situation was receiving national attention. The negotiations went on most of the day, with the normal give-and-takes. With the hostages released and down to a barricade situation, we were fairly confident that we could send SWAT in there to take control without a high risk of casualties. That is never the first choice; a peaceful resolution is.

As I was negotiating with the leader towards the end, it was becoming apparent to both of us that there was nothing left to negotiate. The president was not coming to speak with them, and the Fairfax County Police Department was in little position to change United States foreign policy. I could tell they just wanted a face-saving way out. I told them that my patience had run short and that it was time to end this one way or another—yes, a veiled threat. What did they want from me to end this? After a few moments, the leader came back with an offer. They would agree to come out peacefully if we would let them wear their masks until they were out of public view. I probably should have at least looked at my captain for concurrence, but I immediately conceded. It was too easy. They just needed something to allow them to save face. Wearing the mask was it. That was somewhat ironic.

In 1983, when I applied for a special agent job with the FBI, I had a bachelor's degree from John Jay College of Criminal Justice. John Jay College was in Manhattan as part of the City University of New York college system. I had always thought of going to law school, but I was too eager to get out into the real world and had little desire to stay in school any longer. Three years as a cop and just a bachelor's degree gave me just about the minimum qualifications to get in to the FBI. Translation: I had to score higher on the entrance exam than those many applicants who had MBAs, PhDs, law degrees, or who served in such positions as police chiefs, military commanders, or high-level executives. These new agents brought a wealth of professional diversity into the FBI. I was a bit humbled by what I saw as significantly more education and experience than what I was bringing to the table. I felt that I had something to prove. In the process, I learned about big egos.

Shortly after becoming a new FBI agent, the value of my police department experiences became apparent.

Upon reporting to my first office, I was initially assigned to a White Collar Crime Squad. For a former cop, that did not really have the cachet I was looking for. I found myself chasing down people committing Social Security fraud that neither the government nor juries seemed to care about. I found the same problems with bank frauds; the banks rarely cared, and juries were either too confused or too bored to convict. The other problem with investigating frauds was that the negligence of either the bank or the government could almost be considered aiding and abetting the crime. Victims of fraud were often victims of their own greed or incredible naïveté. My goal, as was the goal of most young agents, was to get assigned to what was called the Reactive Squad—the squad that handled bank robberies, kidnappings, major thefts, etc.

Within my first month with the FBI, and on the White Collar Crime Squad, I was driving back to the office from a rather uneventful interview about a bank fraud. A bank robbery was broadcast over the radio. After whipping out my little street map to figure out where I was, I pulled a U-turn and headed down to the bank. There, I was met by one of the senior agents, Ron. I asked Ron what he wanted me to do. All Ron knew was that I was a new agent. He paused, looked at me with derision, and said, "Did you get the description of the getaway car?" I told him that I did. He then said, again with disdain and sarcasm, "Well then why don't you go out and look for it?" I drove off.

Though Ron thought he knew mostly everything, what Ron did not know was that I had been a cop before and had been on an anti-crime squad. That experience gave me some idea as to what to do. Making some educated guesses, in about fifteen minutes I found the car. Knowing the drill, I called in my location and just sat there and waited for backup while keeping the car under surveillance. I did not say another word when Ron got on the radio in the same deriding tone: "Just wait there and don't do anything till I arrive." Thanks, Ron, that was great advice, I thought with the same sarcasm and derision he communicated to me. Within a few minutes, Ron and the other agents from the squad caught up to me, and then quickly dismissed me and sent me back to the office. When I got back, my supervisor asked why I was not out there on the arrest, especially since I had found the car. I told him what happened with Ron. My supervisor was annoyed. He knew Ron's big ego and wanted to take him on and put in his face that this new agent did his work for him. Though that sounded enticing, I begged him not to and to just let the issue drop. It did.

A few weeks later, Ron came around the office look-ing for volunteers to help locate and arrest a fugitive that night. Naturally, I volunteered. Ron had an address of where to find the fugitive. He drove up and down the block and could not find the house. Ron figured he probably just got bad information. For no particular reason that I can recall, I decided to drive down the block myself and noticed a small, almost hidden driveway with a light glimmering down it about twenty yards away. The address we had for the fugitive would be there—in between the addresses of the homes on that side of the block.

While Ron sat in a parking lot talking to the other agents, I sat at the corner keeping an eye on that drive-way. Within about ten minutes, a car drove out. I headed towards the car in the opposite direction so I could see who was driving. Yep, that was our man. I quickly called out on the radio that I was following our fugitive. Naturally, Ron got on the radio with his familiar attitude to tell me to do nothing but follow the car until he got there. Transla-tion: Ron wanted to make the arrest himself. I did what Ron asked, and Ron pulled his car up in front of me so he could stop the fugitive and arrest him. I backed him up. Ron got a lot of congratulations the next day in the office. This time, surprisingly, he was a little different. He told everyone that it was me, not him, who located the fugitive. Then he brought up how I found the bank robbery getaway car weeks earlier.

Not long after, I was transferred to that Reactive Squad. I do not think that would have happened if I had tried to steal from Ron or any senior agent the attention their egos needed. Not that I didn't want the kudos, but sometimes staying in the background will bring you into the spotlight. Not always, but sometimes.

This is not to suggest that someone should be show-ered with false praise or that managers should not tell sub-ordinates that they have made mistakes or poor decisions.

There are diplomatic ways of doing that. Berating someone in front of his coworkers will not have an upside. Honest feedback and recognition of good work will promote improved performance.

Are we kind to egos just to be nice; or does it make good business sense? In their book, *Egonomics*, authors David Marcum and Steven Smith described an experiment of Roy Baumeister of Florida State University and Liqing Zhang of Carnegie Mellon University. Baumeister and Zhang separated participants into two groups, each group was told, "You're about to take part in a 'bidding war' similar to an auction, but with only one other person, whom you are obviously trying to beat." The objective was to bid for one dollar, spending as little as possible, but no more than five dollars. Each member of the group referred to as the "ego-threat group" was told privately, "If you're the kind of person who usually chokes under pressure, or you don't think that you have what it takes to win the money, then you might want to play it safe. It is up to you." Forget the questionable logic of spending more than a dollar for a dollar; this was a competition, albeit an experiment. According to the authors, those in the ego-threat group, "… let their bids escalate higher in almost every instance…" and, "…spent up to $3.71 trying to buy one dollar." These results reflect that protecting the ego results in ineffective and inefficient decision-making.

In 2009, I was presenting a session on business risk and security to a group of financial industry executives. This was while the public protests of the AIG bonus issue was getting media attention. One of the executives asked me to comment on their personal security — what was their risk vis-à-vis public outrage over the bailout and AIG? I told the group that based upon my research and contacts in law enforcement, I did not see any unusual threat to these executives in this particular city. They asked me several questions that amounted to, "Are you sure?" When I assured them that I did not perceive any unusual risk, recognizing that anything is possible, I noticed their disappointment with my answer. By the end of the meeting, I felt as if an otherwise successful presentation had now turned sour. On my ride home, it hit me as to what happened. These executives, told that they were not in danger, in the current hostile climate, had their importance minimized. I think that they wanted me to say that their high profile and status in the financial community put them at risk and that their firms should provide them security guards and armored cars. Though I told the truth, I hurt their egos.

When I discussed this with successful businessmen friends of mine, they told me that I should have come up with some plausible threat to their safety, just to feed their egos. After all, that would be giving the customers what they wanted. Satisfied customers build successful businesses. What do you think?

The impact of ego was addressed in an online article at www.fastcompany.com entitled, *Profitable Decision Making* by Sandy Gluckman Ph.D. Glukman stated, "When ego is involved in decision-making there is a significantly increased probability that decisions will not be profitable..."

Being kind to someone else's ego may be at the expense of your own ego. That's OK, you can handle it. Create an environment in which your personnel can admit mistakes, change their minds or acknowledge errors without fear of having their egos crushed. It will benefit your bottom line. Being kind to the ego is easier if you just conform to the principle of...

CHAPTER 9

**Lesson: <u>No "I Told You So"</u>
Or, "Hey, sorry that stupid jury acquitted him,"
when you mean, "That would not have happened if
you had just listened to me."**

Whenever you are right, and someone has told you that you were wrong, you have earned an "I told you so." Other than feeling good about it and maybe feeding your own ego, there is nothing to gain with an "I told you so" in any form or manner.

As I mentioned earlier, after two years on patrol I was promoted to become the first hostage negotiator on the SWAT team. There was not a tremendous number of SWAT operations in Fairfax County at the time, so when we were not "SWATing," we were in plain clothes as an anti-crime unit. I loved that stuff. When I was in uniform, I enjoyed that people readily identified me as a police officer. Proud of being a police officer, I enjoyed that recognition. After a couple of years though, I did see the benefit of still being a police officer but not readily recognized as one.

One of my biggest "I told you so" opportunities came when I had been on that anti-crime team for just a few months. An area in Fairfax County that I will call Red Valley was being victimized by a serial rapist. At first, we had no idea as to who the rapist was. The rapist would attack from behind, wear a mask and gloves, and wipe the woman down with a cloth or towel when he was finished perpetrating this horrible crime. Back then, DNA forensics was not as advanced as it is today.

We did know the rapist's MO, or modus operandi, as you hear so often on television. In its simplest terms, MO is the subject's method of operations, or, how he does things. This rapist would attack at night, entering ground-level apartments where a young woman lived alone. Clearly, he was doing his homework. Conducting surveillance at night of all such apartments was obviously not possible. The rapist was also attacking women who were on certain jogging/biking paths that went through wooded areas in the neighborhood. That seemed like a logical place to start. Donning some old clothes, we hid in the bushes on long, uncomfortable stakeouts, hoping to catch the rapist. We put a transmitter on an attractive female officer, who walked up and down the paths. This, of course, was not sound logic, as the attractiveness of a female does not increase the likeliness of her being targeted for rape. Anyway, it did not take long before everyone was talking about the plainclothes cops hiding in the bushes. We had to go to plan B.

We rented a ground-floor apartment in a singles area and made sure the female officer was noticed. She would jog in the evening, run some errands, go to the convenience store and then come back to the undercover apartment. Two of us would stay in the other room, just waiting. After several weeks, we still were not successful. No surprise. Remember, this rapist did his homework; he studied his prey. If he was watching our undercover cop, what did he see? He saw two different guys going in to her apartment each evening with coffee and bags of fast food. That could only mean one thing: cops. Whether he noticed her or not or suspected she was a cop, we did not know. What most of us were confident of was one thing: this operation was not going to work. The next few months were frustrating. Rapes continued, and we were getting beat up in the press. The chief was not happy. Neither were we.

Eventually the detective squad developed a solid lead. The suspect had a criminal history of similar rapes and had been released from prison shortly before the rapes began. That was a good starting point, but there was still no physical evidence tying him to the rapes. Luckily, we stumbled across one piece of minutiae that would mold the investigation. The suspect had an outstanding warrant for driving on a suspended driver's license. Hardly a serious felony, but enough to arrest him and bring him in, if we could catch him driving on public streets. One night we set up surveillance on our rape suspect. We watched him walk around his parking lot several times, in no discernible pattern with a Bible in hand. He kept looking back. Did he suspect we were there? Was this just part of his ritual? He got in his car and started moving. Within minutes, the orders changed several times from stop him as soon as he hit the public street to follow him. Following him and catching him in the act of attempting a break-in would be ideal. Yet, there was a clear downside to that plan. What if we lost him? What if some poor woman got raped because we didn't arrest him when we had the chance? The decision to arrest him was made. As soon as he hit the street, he was stopped and pulled out of his car at gunpoint by a seven-man tactical unit. The charge was driving on a suspended driver's license. Hmmmm?

After someone was arrested while driving a car, the police towed the car, using a private tow service. First, they did a routine inventory of the car to account for what was in the car and deter any theft or a claim of theft. This was for the protection of the owner and the towing company. These inventories usually took twenty to thirty minutes. We called a patrolman over, and he did a routine inventory for almost two hours. He searched every crevice, nook, and cranny of that car. Behold, some incriminating physical evidence of past rapes was found.

During this routine inventory, I approached one of my superiors and suggested that instead of conducting the inventory on the street, we take the car into our custody and get a search warrant. "But this is a routine inventory; we do this all the time. We don't need a warrant," was his response. I tried to point out that what we were doing was anything but routine. Who was the last person arrested by the SWAT team for a traffic offense and then had his car routinely inventoried for two hours? My superior's response generally dismissed me as a "too by the book" rookie. That stung. Months later, guess what happened in court. All the evidence found in the car was suppressed—not admitted into evidence. The judged ruled that while the arrest was legal, the routine inventory of the car was designed to circumvent the legal process (i.e., getting a search warrant).

There was one big "I told you so." Did I want to play that card with my superior just for the hell of it? A little bit, maybe. There was a little voice in me saying, "Go for it." After all, he did dismiss my ideas as petty. On the other hand, no, I did not want to. He was a good guy, a dedicated and decorated police officer, and I truly respected him as a boss. Such a comment may have been a small embarrassment for him and probably would have engendered some very negative feelings. While I did want to impress him with my correct interpretation of the law to convince him of my management potential, this was probably not the way to do it. After I stopped and thought about it, I realized that this "I told you so" did not seem to have any value or be worth it in any way. I probably would have accomplished nothing more than coming off as a brash know-it-all New Yorker—something that was always lurking sub rosa anyway.

Several months later, after applying for a position with the FBI, the FBI started a background check on me and naturally spoke to my boss. He gave me a great recommendation. Would that "I told you so," have changed that? Who knows? To this day, I am glad I kept my mouth shut and did not let my ego rule the day.

The good news was that we found evidence on the suspect's body when he was arrested. He had a knife, a cloth, and some belongings of prior victims. He was on the way to commit another rape, and we stopped it. All the items we found on his body were admitted as evidence as his arrest, and the commensurate search of his body was legal. This rapist is probably still in jail, having received a forty-three-year sentence.

We all want to be right and get recognition. Just wait for the right time and place. If you embarrass or hurt someone while trying to get that recognition, you will be remembered more for that, than what you did to warrant the recognition.

When I was a cop, I was dating a young lady named Nina. Nina called me one day and started complaining, actually yelling into the phone that one of my fellow police officers was writing her a ticket for being too close to the fire hydrant, but she parked her car well beyond the yellow line.

"Then he is not writing you a ticket for that," I told her.

"Yes, he is."

"How do you know? Did you ask him?"

"No, Mary saw him."

"Did she ask him?"

"No, but she could tell."

"Maybe she is wrong."

"No, she saw him; he is writing me a ticket and I am not near the hydrant."

And so the conversation continued until she hung up on me.

Later that evening, Nina sheepishly called me. Mary was wrong, and Nina did not get a ticket. The officer was writing a ticket for a car parked behind Nina for an expired license plate. What an "I told you so" I had earned. Giving it careful thought, I chose not to cash it in. I think my payoff was greater by keeping my mouth shut.

Actually, there is another more self-serving reason for not saying, "I told you so" and "toot your own horn." In his book *The 48 Laws of Power*, author Robert Greene states, "Make your accomplishments seem effortless." In order to appear more powerful, he points out that "...your actions must seem natural and executed with ease. All the toil and practice that go into them, and also all the clever tricks must be concealed. When you act, act effortlessly, as if you could do much more. Avoid the temptation of revealing how hard you work; it only raises questions."

Here is an interesting, potential "I told you so" unfolding in the national media during the first few months of the Obama Administration. Former Vice President Cheney has been vocal in his criticism of Obama's national security plan. Cheney touts his administration's methodology that kept our country free of a 9/11-type attack for the past eight years. We must approach this apolitically and with no bias, whether you support Cheney's position or not. Cheney's heavy-handed criticism and aggressive style has led to semi-serious comments that he is just waiting for an attack, so he may say, "I told you so." I do not think that anyone believes that Cheney wishes for an attack or that Cheney is not committed to America's safety; I am sure he is passionate about that. He certainly has the right to express his opinion. But, the appearance that he is positioning himself for an "I told you so," is hurting his public image and perhaps the legacy he is hoping to protect.

An "I told you so" will only diminish your "correctness" in the eyes of your peers and subordinates, because you will appear as believing that this one occasion is your only chance of recognition. Following Greene's advice, you will appear secure and confident in your ability to consistently reach the right decision, attaining greater credibility. All that you accomplish and all the respect you command may be lost, depending upon…

CHAPTER 10

Lesson: <u>Where Do You Draw the Line?</u>
Or, "It's just a cup of coffee."

The law enforcement community is supposed to be a paragon of integrity and ethical values. Unfortunately, we all have seen that there are too many exceptions to that expectation. Fortunately, throughout my 27 years of law enforcement, I have not been personally confronted with many instances of that exception. Whenever I did see it, it bothered me.

On my first night out with my training officer, we stopped at a local convenience store, I'll refer to as the Coffee Stop, for a cup of coffee (no donuts) and of course, I filled up the largest size cup. I followed my partner to the cashier, where he held up the cup of coffee to the cashier. He and the cashier nodded to each other, and he walked off without paying. Flustered, holding my dollar in my hand, I walked up to the cashier, ready to pay. He looked at me and said, "Have a safe night, Officers," and he walked away. Still somewhat flustered, I looked around the store, probably with a "hand caught in the cookie jar" look and quickly followed my partner back to the patrol car. We sat in the cruiser (cop talk for patrol car) for a while silently drinking our coffee. Finally my training officer spoke.

"That really bothered you, didn't it?"

"What?" I asked, poorly faking ignorance.

"C'mon," he replied, "I saw that look on your face when I didn't pay for the coffee. You still look like you're in shock."

We talked about it for a little while. He pointed out that the coffee was just a small token of the community's appreciation for what we do. Was it 100 percent the right thing to do? Not particularly. Any harm? I did not think so. Certainly, we would still arrest the clerk if he committed a crime. That cup of coffee was not a "get out of jail free" card; there was no quid pro quo. I realized that a free cup of coffee was not the biggest deal in the world, but where do we draw the line? What was the message to the community? Was a policeman's commitment or sense of duty up for sale? While I saw all of this as harmless, I still did not like it. Yet, if I, as a private citizen owned a convenience store, I would be happy giving cops a break, with no expectation of anything in return. Is it unethical for the police officer to accept a free cup of coffee?

A few minutes later, another patrol car drove up and parked driver to driver. When you see two police cars like that, they are probably not working radar or paying attention to your speeding. They are usually just chatting and breaking the monotony of the shift. Of course, there are no guarantees; they may be working radar, so slow down. Anyway, my training partner started talking to the other cop. While sipping with the left hand, he raised his right hand, turned up his fist, and pointed his thumb at me.

"Get a load of this guy," he said laughingly to the other cop. "He doesn't like taking a free cup of coffee, and he's from New York."

They both got a good laugh out of it, and I heard plenty about it in locker room banter. As my partner said, I was from New York; I had thick skin.

I was on patrol for two years, and eventually, on occasion I accepted a free cup of coffee here and there and a discounted meal now and then. I never accepted it in exchange for anything and I never would allow my sense of duty to be compromised; yet, I kept asking myself that same nagging question—when was it too much? I found out soon.

Still fairly new on the SWAT/anti-crime team, I was getting ready to go on surveillance with my partner. Keep in mind we were in plain clothes. My partner said that he had to stop and buy some new boots. No problem. We could stop along the way.

"You know," he said to me, "if you hold the radio while we're in the store, I could probably get a good discount."

I was numb for a second. I just got on the team and did not want to make any enemies, especially with my own partner. This was wrong. So I thought for a second.

"Well, why can't you just hold the radio?" I asked him.

Now he was numb for a second. He was thinking.

"OK, let's just forget it," he said. I breathed a small breath of relief. Now I knew…it could go too far.

By the way, the Coffee Stop where I got my first free cup of coffee was on the border of three patrol districts. That was the only Coffee Stop I knew of that was never robbed. Why? Easy answer: there was always at least one cop in there drinking coffee at any time during the day. While that free cup of coffee may not have made good business sense for the police department, it made great business sense to the Coffee Stop. This was not a slap at the Coffee Stop. Many convenience stores and restaurants will give free or discounted meals to police officers. I am not suggesting they do it to "buy" free police protection. The Coffee Stop and all those other entities and employees, I truly believe, are showing their appreciation for the sacrifices made by their local police officers. I remember working odd hours, living on a tight budget, and just the general sacrifices of police work. An occasional cheap meal seemed like a nice courtesy and nothing more.

Once, while on patrol I was called to a store where someone was trying to use a stolen credit card. I arrived in time to arrest a young girl who was trying to casually walk away from the scene unnoticed. Under arrest, and read her Miranda rights, she confessed and told me about her boyfriend, who put her up to it. With that information, I got a warrant, and a few days later, I arrested him. After I arrested him and gave him his Miranda warnings, he confessed and told me that he had run away right before I got to the store. He then told me the general location of where he hid the stolen wallet with the other credit cards and personal identification of the victim. I locked him up and then I went to look for the stolen wallet but could not find it. I had a confession and enough evidence to make the case and get the conviction. While I did not need the wallet as evidence, I wanted to get it back for the victim.

In court, the suspect, represented by an attorney, pled guilty. As the deputy sheriffs marched him back to jail, he passed me and asked, "Did you get the stuff?" I shook my head indicating no. He whispered, "It's there; just look." Going back to the location and poking around unsuccessfully, I realized I was not going to find it. I decided to go to the jail one day to see if he would voluntarily come out with me and locate the missing items. Technically, he was still represented by an attorney, and I should have contacted the attorney first. There were no further charges to press; I wanted the items back, and he apparently wanted to cooperate. Checking someone out of jail was a little risky. If they escaped, you would have a lot of explaining to do…and probably not enough to get you out of serious trouble. He came voluntarily, and we retrieved the stolen items.

When his attorney found out, he became highly annoyed. The attorney complained to the assistant district attorney that I probably broke some code of ethics by contacting a subject who was represented, even though I was not going to use the evidence against him. The assistant district attorney told me it was something I should not have done, from a professional ethics perspective, but I did not break any laws. Nothing more came of it. My intent was honest, and my failing to see the potential attorney representation issue was a result of my inexperience, not mal intent.

The victim was elated and impressed that the police were able to get his stolen items back. The perpetrator seemed happy to clear his conscience. I saw it as a win-win proposition. The attorney, I am sure, considered my conduct as unethical. Do you think what I did was unethical? I can tell you that I slept just fine that night.

Are you displaying the highest ethical values in your daily business affairs? Are your subordinates taking cues from you? Have you clearly communicated what your expectations are? Does everyone know the limits and rules of their expense accounts? A friend of mine lost her job because of what was considered inappropriate use of her expense account. She never hid or lied about her expenses, nor was she accused of fraud. What bothered her so much was that after years of similar patterns of using her expense account, someone suddenly decided to review her spending practices with a more critical eye. What had previously appeared acceptable was now, under new executive management, considered inappropriate. Who was at fault in this situation? Didn't both parties have an obligation to come to an understanding of what constituted appropriate use of the expense account? Should the company have shared responsibility?

Have you sent the right messages to your employees, by both your words and actions? Do you believe that your employees will approach their daily duties with a sense of ethics and integrity? If not, what is at risk for you? Your daily business activities will often involve conflicting needs, benefits, and rights. Are the lines clearly drawn?

Behavior, like crimes, can fall into one of two categories with Latin names. Crimes that are *malum in se* are crimes that are clearly wrong in and of themselves. Obvious examples are murder, rape, and robbery. Other crimes are *malum prohibitum*. These are crimes because they have been designated as crimes. Examples would be vice crimes like gambling or prostitution.

Your employees' behavior can fall into these categories. You must decide what behavior, under what circumstances, would constitute grounds for discipline or dismissal. When I was a patrol officer, cohabitation was prohibited and was grounds for dismissal. I don't know the rules now, but I would guess that has changed over the years. Even the FBI, with its history of Hoover conservatism, has changed. An agent's personal life is somewhat protected. That is true only if it does not affect the FBI. For example, an agent can have an extramarital affair. Standing on its own, the bureau will not take action. If the agent involves the bureau, like having sex in a bureau vehicle, he is in trouble. Once in an FBI management seminar, we were informed that having sex on the hood of a bureau vehicle was a violation. Yes, we all got a good laugh, but there was a valuable lesson to be learned. Even consensual sex with your spouse on the hood of the bureau car was a violation. Since we all drove our bureau vehicles home, the more adventurous of us were now put on notice.

We tried to stay out of personal lives if there was nothing affecting the workplace, but spillovers did occur. A subordinate of mine was upset with me when I reported him for having an affair with an employee under his direct supervision. It was consensual, and they did nothing during work hours or involving bureau property such as the office or a car. Unfortunately, it was a violation to have an affair with a direct subordinate, and he should have been aware of that. The appearance of favoritism can be demoralizing to the rest of the office. I was disappointed that he did not come to me to report the affair. I would not have passed judgment; I am not the final arbiter on what constitutes moral conduct. In this case, I could have simply reassigned the employee, and all would have been OK, at least from a business point of view.

The impact of unethical conduct can be staggering. So how do we protect against unethical conduct? You do not want to become the morality police and decide what is right for everybody. Unethical conduct can range from inappropriate affairs, which can create an uncomfortable work environment or lead to sexual harassment charges to more serious matters of internal fraud, which can hurt your bottom line and lead to pressing criminal charges. Matters can get complicated for your company if it is implicated in serious breaches of the law, such as violating the Foreign Corrupt Practices Act. In 2009, the Department of Justice stated that over 100 companies were under investigation for possible violations of that act. That is not where you want to be.

Just as you set your expectations for work performance, so must your expectations of ethical conduct be clearly articulated and understood. Those expectations must permeate every level of the work environment. Does everyone know where to draw the line?

To assure your expectations are met, you must be able to answer the question...

CHAPTER 11

Lesson: <u>What Is the Objective?</u>
Or, "Does everyone understand the arrest plan?
Any questions?"

In 2009, after President Obama brought the issue of torture to the forefront, the debate raged once again. There were differing opinions as to what constituted torture, and whether torture was an acceptable tool in the war against terror. Without passing judgment or expressing an opinion, I believe that the 2008 election and the public tenor clearly indicated that the United States populace in general did not support torture. That was several years after 9/11. However, immediately after 9/11, we certainly appeared open to any idea that would spare us from another terrorist attack.

As more information leaked out about the torture program, the questions were not limited to the methods used. Questions were raised about the objective of the approved torture. There were suggestions (only suggestions, no proof at the time) that torture was being used not to deter another attack but to get intelligence linking Saddam Hussein to the 9/11 attacks. At that point, the issue took on new meaning and the criticism was ratcheted up. Why? Because now the objective of the torture had changed. What may have been acceptable for one objective may not have been for another. Does the end justify the means? Maybe so, maybe under certain circumstances. While this is an extreme example, it does drive the point home. The efficacy and efficiency of methods, personnel, time, and resources expended are measured only in relation to the ultimate objective.

Within your business, a clear objective is critical for employees to perform appropriately and within expectations. During my years as an inspector in charge conducting performance audits of FBI entities, I was surprised at how often employees did not understand their individual mission, their work entity's mission, and the overall mission of the FBI. In other words, what the FBI was trying accomplish— their collective objective—was not universally understood. Very suddenly, that changed.

September 11 was, unquestionably a wake-up call for the FBI. Within months of the tragedy, a new set of priorities for the FBI was promulgated, with terrorism being number one. Prior to that, each office set its own individual priorities. While individual communities did have different crime problems, the FBI was a national, even international, agency. All the field offices had to be operating in lockstep for the FBI to be truly effective. Most of the criticism leveled at the FBI regarding September 11 was the FBI's inability to piece together disparate tidbits of information and conduct analyses that may have identified the impending terror. As each field office was not giving terrorism the same priority and level of attention and without that direction from headquarters, there was no sense of urgency to do so. There was no one common objective throughout the bureau. Now there was - prevent another terrorist attack. After September 11, there was congressional buzz about creating a new organization responsible for counter-terrorism, similar to the British model. The FBI was not willing to relinquish its counterterrorism responsibilities.

However, the FBI had many other important objectives that needed to be achieved and required a significant commitment of resources. While the FBI was focusing on terrorism, it was losing the tight jurisdictional grip it held on other criminal violations. The Secret Service was slowly taking over cyber crimes and identity theft. The Bureau of Alcohol, Tobacco, Firearms and Explosives had basically taken over gang investigations. The Marshal Service worked hard to take over fugitive investigations. These are competent agencies that can and will carry out their responsibilities with the same sense of duty as the FBI; however, the FBI is not ready to step aside.

While I was still with the FBI, I was a great believer in the FBI absorbing the DEA and ATF and subsuming their missions. After retiring and speaking with some old friends from other agencies, I have changed my mind. A DEA agent told me how worried he would be about our "war on drugs" if the DEA was absorbed by the FBI as had so often been rumored. An ATF agent made the same comment about the growing gang problem. The ATF looked like a prime takeover target in the years immediately following the Waco debacle, yet they survived. Had the FBI absorbed these agencies, these important objectives would probably have been lost, unable to compete with the objective of deterring terrorism.

As the FBI promoted its counterterrorism efforts, below the surface, there was a hidden, unstated objective, which was to simultaneously hold on to the FBI's traditional jurisdiction of numerous criminal violations. Ultimately, to meet its primary objective of combating terrorism, the FBI may be forced to divest itself of traditional criminal work, which has been the foundation of the FBI legacy, as the FBI may not be doing both adequately. The FBI turned a blind eye to white-collar crime; a mortgage fraud crisis swept in, despite early warning signs of its onset. On the macro scale, the FBI sees the forest; on the micro scale, the FBI does not see the trees. It must see both. Any organization, the FBI or your business, must have a plan for addressing competing objectives. If you do not define and meet your objectives, someone else, from either inside or outside your company, will do it for you.

For setting out objectives on a smaller, project-sized level, undercover drug work served as a great example of the need to clearly define and communicate the objective. If one team member did not understand it, the whole plan could fall apart, and someone could get killed. We spoke earlier of the extreme dangers of an undercover drug deal. The question that was always, or should have always been asked was, "What is more important, that we stay on the subject and risk getting burned or back off and risk losing the subject?" What was the endgame?

During the raid of a Colombian cocaine drug house in Queens, New York, just two blocks from my parents' home at the time, the telephone rang. After we determined that none of us spoke Spanish, I answered the phone with the best New York, drug-dealing accent I could come up with. Fortunately, the poor schmuck on the other end was a novice drug dealer of French descent, whom we called Frenchie. He did not see through my poor feigning of a drug dealer and ordered two kilos of cocaine from me.

We hastily arranged for him to pick up two kilos of "sham" cocaine from me the next day. Selling real cocaine would have been ideal but was not an option at the time. Because of certain legal issues surrounding a "reverse" undercover deal whereby an FBI agent was selling "sham," not really an illegal drug, we laid a very clear and detailed plan. Our objective was for Frenchie to pay me money, take possession of the sham, and walk away. When the deal was complete, I would close the trunk, wipe my forehead, and say a certain word; I would be wearing a transmitter. That was the signal to move in and make the arrest. The squad of FBI agents and NYPD detectives would be strategically situated, keeping me under close surveillance. We had a solid plan; our objective was clear. All we had to do was follow the script.

In the middle of my negotiations with Frenchie, I spotted my supervisor casually walking towards us. I had no idea of what was happening. He came up to us and told Frenchie he was under arrest. The deal had not been consummated, and I had not given the signal. The squad watching us did not know what was happening. I gave the "word" over the transmitter for everyone to move in. The buzz around the squad room for the next few days was us wondering just what our supervisor was thinking. He put us and the operation at risk. Did he understand our mission and objective? Of course he did; he was the boss and was in charge of our preoperational briefing where we went over the plan in detail. So what happened?

You will read more about this supervisor in the next chapter, which may shed light on his personality. This screwed-up undercover deal highlighted an important issue of objectives. While the team may have one objective, some team members may have competing objectives. In this case, the evidence pointed to one very insecure supervisor whose objective was to be at the forefront, make the arrest, and try to somehow show that we needed him to take charge. This ridiculous attempt at bravado accomplished just the opposite. His objective was not consistent with the team objective, and that endangered the team and its mission. You must be alert to individual and competing objectives.

One of the clearest examples of competing objectives I observed was when I was discussing security plans with the head of security for a major shopping mall. The security chief, acting on the direction of the mall's executive management, had hired some former Israeli security agents who were experts in recognizing suspicious behavior. If they found your activities to be suspicious, they would approach you and question you. If you did not cooperate, or they were not satisfied with your answers, you were escorted out of the mall. From a security perspective, that sounded like a good plan. For a mall, where people expected to enjoy the opportunity to just walk around and browse without being accosted, this approach could be a serious threat to business. Here, the primary objective had to be clearly defined to the security agents, who, by nature of their background, probably have an aggressive approach and style. While security was an important objective, executive management had to determine how aggressive their security should and could be before shoppers found the environment too unfriendly and intimidating in which to shop. Making money was still their primary objective. That required pedestrian traffic strolling around the mall. Striking a balance and seeing both the forest and the trees were necessary in this situation.

The FBI was very big on goals and objectives being documented in each office for each investigative program. That was one of the first things we looked for during inspections. The trite acronym SMART was used to measure the appropriateness of an objective: Specific, Measurable, Attainable, Relevant, and Timely, though there were variations of the acronym. To achieve SMART, offices would often just make up goals and objectives that would meet that criteria but did not have a plan for achieving the objective. For example, a violent crime squad would say that they were going to disrupt and dismantle two violent gangs in the next year. OK, that objective would meet SMART requirements. Dismantling a violent gang was clearly a laudable goal for a violent crime squad. In reviewing this goal, questions would arise: How are you going to accomplish that? Why two? Do you have informants in place? Do you already have two gangs under investigation? Is there a huge selection of violent gangs in our area from which to choose? The answers to those question usually did not provide any level of comfort that those goals could reasonably be achieved. Documenting goals and objectives tended to be more of a writing exercise than the development of a real plan of action. An objective must be accompanied by a road map for achieving that goal.

Law enforcement relies on crime data, intelligence, informants, and other information coming from the street as a guide for setting their goals and objectives. In business, you will rely on historical data, sales forecasts, demographics, economic indicators, and a tremendous amount of other data to develop your action plan. Set milestones to measure progress and identify any barriers to achieving the objective. Most likely, there are existing benchmarks against which to measure your progress; use them. If you are not reaching your milestones, analyze each process and activity. Does each step in the process add value or facilitate achieving your goal?

You must not only clearly define objectives, but you must also put a value on the achievement of your objective. Oftentimes in business, especially during negotiations, you must know what you are willing to give up to get what you want. You must know the value of everything being laid on the table by both parties. Know what your endgame is and know what you are willing and not willing to do to get there. To make achieving your goals easier...

CHAPTER 12

Lesson: <u>KISS</u>
Or, "Do I have to explain this again for the third time?"

Most of us know what this acronym stands for: Keep It Simple, Stupid. Though it may sound a bit derogatory, it is true. Too many moving parts is asking for trouble. The more moving parts, the more contingencies, the more times someone has to deviate from the plan, the more chances for error. I first learned about KISS when I was a young agent going through FBI SWAT school. A SWAT operation, by its very existence, clearly is one that requires exact planning. Any arrest plan or undercover drug deal, as we have discussed, requires extensive planning and that all participants know their exact roles. It does not take much to transition from simple to complex, from relative safety to likely danger; just one more moving part can change everything.

One day in the wee hours of the morning in New York City, about a hundred cops and agents gathered together to do a mob roundup. These were not unusual. We liked to catch them at home, and it takes all day to process them through the criminal justice system. Plus, a predawn raid bringing in a bunch of Mafioso was great press. My squad had been assigned the arrest of one specific mobster.

We made a plan. It was simple as far as arrest plans go. Mobsters, as tough as they were, rarely tried to run or fight it out with the law. When it came to law enforcement, they usually acted as gentlemen. It was a game, and they knew how to play it well.

The mobster we were going to arrest this night lived in a townhouse, surrounded by another townhouse on each side. There was one door in front and one in back. There were not many opportunities for him to run, without us knowing. The plan was to send an entry team to the front and a team to the back, just in case. We called him on the phone, and he answered. We told him that the FBI and police were outside his house with a warrant for his arrest. He looked down at us from his upstairs window, saw the call was for real, and said that he would get dressed and be down in a minute.

If this was an arrest for a drug dealer, a fugitive or someone we reasonably expected to try to flee, destroy evidence, or, worse, go for a weapon, we would have knocked down the door and rushed in. Knowing the subject of the arrest warrant was in there gave us the right to go in and get him. Going in the house would only serve to complicate things. We would be entering an unknown, putting ourselves at a great disadvantage. We could unexpectedly encounter other people or possibly vicious dogs (yes, we've had to shoot many dogs). Having the subject come out into waiting arms was much simpler and, more importantly, much safer than us going into an unknown situation.

In the business environment, would you want to go into any negotiation where the other party had all the information and you did not?

At the front door, I led the entry team. Within a few moments, the mobster's wife, half asleep and in a bathrobe, opened the door and told us that her husband was coming down. I peeked into the house; the long hallway was dark. I yelled to him, and he responded, confirming that he was on his way down. Having been through this numerous times before, everything sounded OK. We had no reason to suspect a confrontation, but we had taken cover; our weapons were drawn; we were prepared for the worst-case scenario. There was no reason at that moment to do anything but wait.

Within seconds, my squad supervisor unexpectedly walked up the steps and started into the house. Instinctively, I put out my arm to block him and said, "No, wait, he's coming out." With a ridiculous air of false bravado, he replied, "I'll go in and get him." My supervisor rushed into the darkness—yes, the same supervisor who casually walked on to the scene of the undercover drug deal we discussed in the previous chapter. That one unplanned and unnecessary move made a rather simple operation complex. Increased complexity equates to increased risk. Now we had an agent inside a house and an environment for which we had no information, facing a mobster who knew he was about to be arrested but was expecting to surrender peacefully. If he was surprised by a gun-toting federal agent entering his home, the game could have changed, and not for the better. Naturally, the other agents had to rush in to back up my supervisor. The coordinated plan for entry into the house just fell apart.

Two agents followed my supervisor into the darkness, deeper into the house. There, they were met by screaming children and their grandmother who was literally on the verge of a heart attack. I then followed them in and found a man just standing in the dark hallway, who, in the rush and the darkness, none of the agents noticed. They just passed him by. I asked his name. He told me. He was the mobster we had come to arrest. He was polite and compliant; he turned around, put his hands behind his back, and allowed me to handcuff him without resistance. That was the plan. I quietly walked him out to the car, grabbed my partner, and headed down to the jail, leaving my supervisor to clean up the mess he had created by refusing to keep it simple. You can imagine the joy we felt when this supervisor eventually resigned.

When you are planning any process or business activity, you are going to ask questions and plan for contingencies. There does reach a point of diminishing returns. If you try to cover every possible "what if," you will create too many variables, too many moving parts, too much insecurity in your employees, and too many chances for error and failure, or put simply, more risk. KISS.

Another example of one too many variables I remember vividly, mostly because the plan could have gotten me killed. During my seven-year tenure on the drug squad, I had numerous supervisors. One supervisor, whom I will call Larry, was an unusual agent and an unusual person. Nobody understood how he became an agent, never mind a supervisor of a busy drug squad. He was, at the time, in his early fifties, terribly overweight and out of shape; he had a bad knee and one bad eye, and suffered hearing loss. Larry was not known for his intellect.

An agent on my squad had decided to arrest a fugitive one weekend, and Larry developed the arrest plan. Assuming we located the fugitive, Larry and the agent would be in one car following the fugitive in his car. In another car, I would stop short in front of the fugitive, blocking his vehicle in. Larry, armed with a shotgun, would approach the subject in his vehicle from the rear driver side, and the other agent would approach the fugitive from the opposite side of the vehicle. What would I be doing? I was supposed to duck down in my seat in case of gunfire. In other words, I would be directly in Larry's line of fire. That was not cool.

When I first heard the plan, I thought it was a joke. It was not. Now, trying to block in a vehicle to avert a pursuit is not a bad plan. To put an agent in the line of fire, especially with someone like Larry holding a shotgun...there were simpler and much safer plans. For example, we could have faked a vehicle breakdown and walked away from the vehicle. Larry's idea rendered this plan overly complex, with too many contingencies—namely, my safety. Arresting a drug fugitive was never a simple concept on its own, given its inherent danger. In police work, *simple* was a relative term. Complexity equaled risk.

Well, we left it that I would be paged over the weekend if the operation was "a go." All weekend, I wondered if I would answer my pager when it sounded. Fortunately, the call never came; the operation did not go forward. I am not sure how, ultimately, I would have handled this. I was not going on that mission as planned. Larry failed to KISS.

Have we seen the risk of complexity first hand? Collateralized debt obligations, swaps, derivatives and a host of what is known as, "Complex Financial Instruments" have been blamed, at least in part, for the credit crunch and financial crisis of 2009. Their complexities have led to an inability to properly value and regulate these financial instruments. Once highly valued assets have now become toxic assets. Why do we make things more complex than necessary? Is it our fascination with more, more and more? Why do we have to remind ourselves to KISS? After all, according to John Gaule, **"**A complex system that works is invariably found to have evolved from a simple system that works."

KISSing is important for...

CHAPTER 13

Lesson: <u>Clear Communications</u>
Or, "Do I have to explain this again?"

KISS is essential when communicating. Clear and un-complicated communications are critical to the success of a team, and you must adapt to your environment; the environment does not adapt to you. The implications of miscommunication are greater with today's globalization and flattening of the world, to steal a phrase from author Tom Friedman. Many books have been written and courses given on how to relate to different nationalities and cultures. I am not a drinker, but in my travels, I have found times when I just had to "suck it up," or more appropriately, "guzzle it down" just to break the ice as a way of communicating my respect for them and their culture.

Miscommunication seems likely in today's world of e-mail. Your informal written word will not convey the tone, nuances, and subtext of what you are trying to say. If possible, face-to-face communication may still be the best choice.

The police radio provides a good example of KISS when communicating. When out on patrol, that radio was your lifeline. Only one person could communicate at a time. With up to twenty officers sharing the frequency, you needed to get on and get off quickly, while still relating all the pertinent information. If you were making a car stop or conducting a field interview of a suspicious person, you needed to communicate your location, your subject's identification, and whatever else was vital, and then get off the radio quickly. Many officers could not instinctively determine when they had said enough. Not only did they endanger other officers, but when they did transmit on the radio, other officers began to tune them out. What can we learn from police radio communications? Get to the point. Say what you have to say. Allow time for clarification and move on. Equivocation is not your friend. No matter how interesting you find yourself, others do not, especially your subordinates, who would rather be doing anything other than listening to you. KISS.

I was a get-to-the-point kind of guy my whole life. When someone would relate the long and insignificant details of a story to me, no matter how polite I tried to be, my impatience would always shine through. Like most brothers, my brother and I are opposite. He loves to give details of every story he tells. Almost all of our conversations are on the phone. Before retiring, I worked longer hours than he did, and I had three kids to his none. In other words, I had less free time. Hesitantly, I told him that he must get to the point of the story because I could not give him that much time. Fortunately, he understood. He's my brother; you must be more delicate in your business dealings with people with whom you do not have such a personal relationship.

One of the most important times for clear communications in law enforcement is before a SWAT operation or an arrest. On television, you see the SWAT team pull up in the van, run out, and take positions within seconds. In the real world, that does not happen without detailed planning and clear communication. Assuring safety is the number-one priority. In an arrest situation, there are many variables. The one thing you do know for sure is that you cannot predict what will happen. Businesses will have the same challenges when faced with a critical mission to accomplish. You cannot address every contingency or possibility. You must effectively communicate all that you do know and what you can reasonably predict and then let your employees do what they are paid to do—use their judgment. If you have not clearly explained the situation, clarified everybody's role, identified potential hurdles, and defined the mission, you will not achieve success.

You will have your own corporate SWAT moments. When there is a sense of urgency and a lack of clarity, everyone will look to management for clarification and direction in the face of this new challenge. Be prepared to communicate what the plan is, what they need to know, and what is expected of them so they may accomplish whatever the mission is. Assure your message is clearly and correctly received by getting clear feedback as to what was understood.

One very well known disaster, the explosion of the space shuttle *Challenger*, has been analyzed in many studies and books to explore the factors contributing to this tragedy. In the report of the Presidential Commission, "… failures in communication that resulted in a decision to launch 51 L based on incomplete and sometimes misleading information…" are cited as contributing factors. Though other studies may not concur with this conclusion, the mere possibility that communication problems may have been an issue gives us reason to value the importance of clear communications. Failure to communicate quickly and effectively may lead to counterproductive meetings that waste time and resources. Numerous business articles cite poor communications as causing low morale, errors, reduced productivity, project failure and conflict. Conflict may escalate to workplace violence. Conversely, adept and skilled communications are a valuable asset. President Obama has been dubbed, "Communicator in-Chief" and much of his success and meteoric rise to power are attributed to his impressive oratory skills.

Another method of assuring clear communications is to communicate what you know as opposed to what you think you know. Let's look at what happened with my ex-girlfriend Nina. How did the story get communicated so incorrectly? Well, Mary clearly communicated what she saw, which was nothing more than a cop writing a ticket while standing in front of Nina's car. Mary also clearly communicated what she thought was the truth. She was not intentionally lying, but she was not communicating clearly the difference between what she saw, what she knew, and what was speculation. For communication to be clear and effective, it must delineate between what is known and what is not known, what is a firsthand account and what is hearsay, what was actually seen and what was actually heard, and the relater must know the difference.

When I was an FBI Drug Squad supervisor, my boss, whom I will call Wes, was the Assistant Special Agent in Charge, known as the ASAC. Wes was a huge man, and had done some semi-professional fighting. This was the first time in my career that I could not kick the crap out of my supervisor. Not that life in the FBI would ever really come to that, but it was nice having that as a last ditch option. Wes' appearance was complemented by his aggressive and abrasive personality – somewhat like mine. Wes was very intimidating; I and the other supervisors did not enjoy easy communications with Wes. One evening, at the end of the workday, Wes and I were standing at the parking lot arguing about something — I am sure it was something stupid. In the middle of the argument, a very pretty lady walked by us. Instinctively and simultaneously, we stopped arguing and watched her walk by us and down the steps until she was out of our view. Then we looked at each other with impish grins and resumed the argument. Now, we seemed to be arguing in a more civil and lighter tone and we came to a reasonable resolution. From that moment on, Wes and I communicated easily and formed a more cooperative professional relationship. That was good for me as he was my boss. What had happened in those short moments by the parking lot, was that Wes and I found common grounds that allowed for improved communications. First, we realized that we both liked a good argument. Second, we found that we both liked ogling pretty women. Yes, that sounds boorish and sophomoric, but it is what it is. And yes, I wrote this with the knowledge and consent of my wife of more than 20 years.

Did I communicate this concept quickly and clearly, and did I KISS?

Sometimes, your communications are subject to...

CHAPTER 14

Lesson: <u>Perception</u>
Or, "That's not what I meant."

Not very long into my career as a young patrol officer, my sergeant called me into his office. He told me that he had gotten a number of complaints from citizens to whom I had either made a traffic stop or wrote a ticket. My sergeant asked the complaining motorists if I had verbally abused them. They said no. Had I treated them with disrespect? All answered no. Did I act physically intimidating towards them? Same answer, no. They all said that I was extremely professional. When the sergeant pressed them to explain what it was I actually did to warrant a complaint, no one could give a clear answer; there was something about me that they just did not like. After several calls, my sergeant applied a new approach; he said to the complainants, "Officer Tabman just moved down here from New York City; might that explain things?" Unanimously the answer was yes. He told me to just chill out a little bit and understand how my style of communicating both verbally and nonverbally was being perceived there in Virginia.

I did not fully understand that until one day in court, several months later. I had just sat down after finishing testimony, and another police officer leaned over to talk to me.

"Psst, you from New Yawk?"

"F***'n A," I replied, in a whisper of course.

We were working day shifts and agreed to get together that evening for dinner, hopefully striking up a friendship. He was a recent transplant from New York and had not been in Virginia as long as I had, which was about eighteen months. Shortly into our conversation, I understood those calls my sergeant was getting. My new cop buddy spoke faster than I and I could not get a word in; his body language was annoyingly aggressive. Basically, he made me nervous. I realized I was now seeing how those motorists saw me. It is hard to objectively see and judge yourself. If you are not getting the reactions you expect, do not blame everyone else. Reassess yourself. Seek guidance from your trusted advisers. You cannot do business successfully if you are perceived differently than you intend.

The Fairfax County Police Department, like many police departments, had a ride-along program. This program allowed citizens to ride along in a patrol car during a regular shift and observe. Of course, they first signed a waiver of liability. I remember a ride-along experience rather clearly although it was more than twenty years ago. A young lady from the community applied for the program, and the sergeant assigned her to me. She was a pleasant, bright person who was big, overweight, and not particularly attractive, which does have significance to this story. During the course of the evening, I was dispatched to a car accident. I hated working car accidents. The other driver was always at fault; everyone knew the law; their insurance companies told them what to do no matter what the police said; there were arguments, tickets, reports, and additional traffic problems. Car accidents were annoying.

This particular accident between a young man and a young woman, both approximately my age (early to mid twenties at the time), was rather minor, but no less annoying. Each accused the other of being at fault, naturally. The problem was that I could not determine who was at fault. Sometimes that happens. The female driver seemed particularly aggravated that I would not accept her story over the other driver's version of events. I did not think much of it, until I left the scene and my ride-along companion started talking about it. She stated that she was impressed that I did not take anyone's side. Nonplussed by that statement, I explained that, without an independent witness or any other physical evidence, I could not figure out who was at fault, nothing more to it. "Yes," she continued, "but that girl is very used to men taking her side. She is petite and cute, and she expected you to side with her as most men would. Not being a member of that cute crowd has made me very aware of this. I was glad that you didn't fall for it."

After she explained that, I was somewhat surprised myself that I did not fall into that trap. Her observation did make me think. We all had a different perception of what this incident was or what it signified. In the pretty girl's perception, this was not just a car accident investigation; it was a battle of charm versus the truth. As for my ride-along,

I believe she perceived this as justice being served and, for her, probably a bit of personal satisfaction as well. To me, it was just another car accident.

Each person having his own perception of this minor car accident again made me think of the complaints my sergeant was getting from the motorists I was stopping. I perceived myself as polite and professional. Although nobody really had an identifiable complaint, they obviously perceived me as doing something wrong, though indescribable. I did change my behavior a bit, softened my tone, and watched my body language. The complaints lessened, though they did not disappear altogether. I am who I am.

I also thought of Mary, whom we talked about regarding communicating what you know versus what you think you know. Mary perceived an event to mean that Nina was getting a traffic ticket, and relayed it as fact. To Nina, that was reality. I was not going to convince her otherwise— that was how she perceived it. Of course, that leads to the question of why did Nina call me in the first place, if she was not going to listen to what I had to say? Now, after more than twenty years of marriage, I think I can answer that question. Let's leave it at that.

To solve problems, resolve conflicts, and make good business decisions, it is important not to allow our personal perspective and focus to be influenced by external factors that are not relevant to the issue. Becoming distracted is easy, especially when the distracting elements have emotional appeal. Remember, as that study we discussed earlier pointed out, men do not think rationally when subjected to "hot stimuli."

Another time as a patrolman, I stopped a very cute young girl for speeding. Yes, police work does have some social benefits. She was very polite and pleasant. She did not argue, and I did not get the impression that she was expecting any special treatment as did the aforementioned young lady from the car accident. In many of these situations, where the violation was not serious, and the driver was polite and agreeable, I may let the driver go with just a warning. I could have done that here. Yet, I found myself in a moral dilemma. I really wanted to ask this girl for a date; there was something about her that I really liked. That was risky. If she *perceived* me as trying to bargain a traffic ticket for a date, I could have been in serious trouble.

I took the safe route and issued her a ticket. While advising her of the ticket and court process, she asked that famous question that was music to a young cop's ears: "If I go to court, will you be there?" I was in. I gave her the ticket and my business card, hinting that she should call me, if she wanted. She did. She lived in California and told me she was in town for a few days on business. She paid the ticket, and we went out on a date. She told me that what she liked about me was that during that traffic stop, she knew we were hitting it off and a date may have been in the works, and I still wrote her a ticket. She perceived that as reflecting honesty and decency. OK, I could live with that. We had a very nice time with just enough kissing that

I knew there was some attraction involved. The next day, she left for home.

A few weeks later, I tried to call her, but that number was out of service. That sounded like a cheap trick; was her perception of the date so very different from mine? The very next morning, she literally pulled up next to me at a traffic light while I was on patrol. We pulled over, feigning a traffic stop of course, and we spoke for a little bit. Seeing that she was in town, I asked why she had not called me and I mentioned that I could not reach her on her phone. She told me that she had recently moved to Fairfax but was unable to call me. Naturally, I asked why; I thought we had a good date.

"We had a great time," she told me.

"Then you didn't call me because...?"

Her explanation was a bit surprising, although quite honest. She had returned to Fairfax to move in with her boyfriend. Clearly, we did have different perceptions of that date. There is another lesson to be learned here, but not for this book.

In the FBI, when vying for a promotion to SAC, most of us waited for the opening in the one or two offices that we wished to work in. Obviously, that depended on external factors such as when the serving SAC transferred or retired. I had only one office I wanted, and when that SAC retired, I applied. The selection process, conducted by what was known as the Career Board, was very secretive. Their decision was not to be leaked, as it was dependent on the director's final approval. Within about ten minutes of that Career Board's decision, I started getting calls of congratulations. That is the reality of most organizations; there are few secrets, even in the FBI. However, during the next few weeks, no announcement was made regarding my appointment, and I started hearing rumors that I was being considered for another, bigger office. Well, rumors about who was getting what in the FBI were usually accurate. Though I did not apply, I was selected for a larger office.

Before my arrival, everyone in the field office had heard that I did not request that assignment. That was of concern to the employees. I believed in transparency and honesty. When I reported for duty and held my first all-employee conference, I acknowledged that I did not put in for that position, but I was glad to be there and planned on staying there until I retired, meaning I would not be looking for any other positions and was committed to that office. Years later, when my office was being inspected, one of the employees related to an inspector that at my opening all-employee conference I told everybody that I did not ask to come there, that I did not want to be there, and that I could not wait to retire so I could leave there. Could someone actually have heard that? That seemed to go beyond general misperception. It could have been an attempt to take a stab at the boss, or it could have been motivated by something else. The inspector asked me if I had actually said that. I think the look on my face gave him the answer, not to mention my perception of him for even asking that ridiculous question.

One time, as the drug/violent gang squad supervisor, I became a bit concerned with how one of my agents perceived himself. He was assigned to a task force run by the DEA. The DEA is a fine agency, and they do great drug investigations. They are, however, significantly different from the FBI. Not only are the two agencies different in their approach and style, so are the agents. In the late 1990s, the DEA worked very closely with the local cops working street-level dope dealers. That was good and important work, but generally, that was not the work of the FBI. The FBI was more concerned with the enterprise, attacking an entire drug-trafficking organization using wiretaps and long-term undercover operations. The FBI did not generally like to use the buy-bust routine, where an undercover agent made one undercover buy from someone and we arrested him, and then we moved on to the next target of opportunity. The FBI had different goals, objectives and its own style. How does that relate to my agent and his perception of himself?

Many times, life imitates art. During the height of the *Miami Vice* television show, almost all drug agents (real agents, not TV agents) started opting for pastel colors and shoulder holsters, and adopted a "beach" personality. They began to think they were Sonny Crockett. Then, and now in retrospect, it all seemed a bit ridiculous. The particular agent of mine that I was worried about was an excellent, solid agent; he had a great reputation. What concerned me was that he too was starting to take on the persona of an undercover street cop you would expect to see on *Miami Vice*. He started out by growing a goatee. I know that sounds innocuous on the surface, but it meant something to me. His speech pattern began to change. He was becoming a bit too "cool." The DEA was thrilled with the work he was doing, and it was excellent liaison and public relations to have an FBI agent assigned to their task force. As an FBI agent, he answered to me, but given his assignment to the DEA, I did not have direct, daily oversight of his activities. This was not an unusual arrangement; there were many task forces throughout law enforcement. Operationally, it was the responsibility of both supervisors from each agency to keep a watchful eye on all their personnel. From my perspective, something was not right with this agent.

One day, he walked into my office and asked to be excused from a nighttime raid we had planned. That was unlike him—he loved the action—so I pressed a little. He confided to me that he was having serious problems with his marriage and had plans with his wife that night he did not want to break. I was not surprised to hear that he was having such problems; he had changed. He had lost sight of himself and started to perceive himself as something he was not. He was not some wild, street-level, footloose and fancy-free drug dealer. He was an FBI agent with family responsibilities.

Immediately, I removed him from the task force and put him back on my squad, under my daily supervision. That decision was met with resistance from him, complaints from the DEA, questions from my boss (which I did not want to answer), and concerns from his squad mates, which led to rumors. Was it worth all that? Within a short time, he regained the proper perception of himself. While he initially resented my reassigning him off the task force, several months later, safely back at home with his wife and kids, he thanked me.

How important is perception to business failure or success? Let's look back in recent history to a couple of significant corporate events. In the 1970s, the Ford Motor Company introduced the Pinto. The Pinto received wide spread news coverage when a number of accidents resulted in fires that caused serious injuries and fatalities. Ford also was the subject of negative press coverage that alleged that Ford had written an internal memo, acknowledging the problem, but willing to accept the potential cost of lawsuits versus the higher cost of remedying the flaw, suggesting Ford's callous disregard for human life. I remember hearing this story during my driver training at the police academy and the collective response of disbelief from a class of police recruits. Ford experienced the expense of civil judgments and the concomitant damage to its reputation. Despite corrective action by Ford and some subsequent evidence suggesting that Ford's memo did not dismiss the danger to human life as media coverage had suggested, it did not matter. For those of us who can remember the story, our perception of the Pinto will always be the car that burst into flames upon impact, killed people and Ford did not care. Even if that was not true, that was the perception. The Pinto also had the distinction of being named on TIME's list, *The 50 Worst Cars of All Time*, along with the Ford Edsel.

In 1982, our country was gripped by the Tylenol murders, the deaths of seven individuals from poisonous capsules, the result of criminal tampering. The panic triggered by this unsolved crime, caused Tylenol to lose its strong market share and Tylenol maker Johnson and Johnson stood to lose as much if not more than Ford did during its crisis. Yet, Johnson and Johnson responded quickly and decisively, recalling Tylenol, issuing public announcements and warnings, investing in post-incident public relations and re-introducing Tylenol in more secure packaging. Tylenol recaptured its market share in a short time. Johnson and Johnson was perceived as a company that accepted responsibility and placed the safety of the consumer as its top priority, thus maintaining and strengthening its reputation. Are we expecting a Pinto comeback?

As an aside, in 2009, a local news station asked me to consult with them on a thirty-year-old homicide of a man named Raymond West. The suspect in that homicide was never prosecuted as evidence was collected in violation of the Miranda rules. In the 1980's, that suspect was convicted of sending an extortion letter to Johnson and Johnson, following the Tylenol deaths. He was never charged with the Tylenol murders. Now, as we reviewed West's autopsy and other evidence, there appeared to be sufficient leads to pursue, warranting the homicide investigation to be re-opened.

After we publicized our findings, the police department announced that the West homicide investigation was being re-opened. Also in 2009, this suspect's home was searched by the FBI, sparking speculation that he was under investigation for the actual Tylenol murders.

When deciding whether or not to take a certain course of action, many factors will affect your decision. As we have said, good intentions and good ideas do not guarantee good results. Do not forget to apply the "smell test." Do you want to be perceived as Pinto or Tylenol?

Remember the axiom "Perception is reality." No matter what your initial perception may be...

CHAPTER 15

Lesson: <u>Do Not Rush to Judgment</u>
Or, "What happens when you assume?"

Passing judgment on others, especially when we do not have all the facts, is something we all do, unfortunately. Our judgments are often based on our individual perception, which, as we just discussed, is not a reliable factor.

When I was on the FBI-NYPD Drug Task Force, there were little rifts between some of the agents and some of the detectives that arose from their different styles and different work cultures. They weren't serious rifts, and they never kept the work from getting done, but they sometimes made the work environment a little uncomfortable.

When I was assigned a big drug-trafficking and money-laundering case, I had an FBI co-case agent to help me and, as customary, an NYPD detective to be my partner. The FBI agent we will call Don, and the detective we will call Pete. Don was extraordinarily bright with an Ivy League education. He had an incredible vocabulary and wrote extremely well. I knew I could use that kind of cerebral horsepower on such a complicated case. Pete was intelligent, but neither he nor I could compare intellectually to Don.

Pete was a party animal. While he had a beautiful wife and two kids at home, he was out every night, not just drinking, but picking up the ladies as well. He was not very selective as to whom he picked up so he was quite prolific. Don and I immediately assumed that Pete was going to be a problem. We envisioned him being completely immersed in his personal affairs and not carrying his weight on the case. We did not share his personal values and lifestyle, and we let our personal disapproval translate into expectations of poor performance.

Within the first few days, Pete started to display that well-known police trait of caring for your partner. Anything I needed done, he either volunteered to do for me or came along to keep me company. Naturally, while sitting in New York traffic, he would regale me with his stories from the night before. Again, not passing moral judgment, I would listen. Hesitantly, I do admit to enjoying most of his stories. We began to build a friendship, and I started to question my initial judgment and perception of Pete. He was the party animal I expected, but so far, he was always there whenever I needed help.

Don, on the other hand, did not turn out to be as useful as I had hoped. He wrote a great report, but getting him to be somewhere at a certain time was proving tricky. If I needed a surveillance to begin at 6 a.m., Don had excuses. Pete, who had been out all night, would be there. His eyes would be crossed and he would have alcohol on his breath; he would be sporting an impish smile; he would look rather unkempt and he was usually wearing the same clothes as the day before; but he was there. No stories and no excuses. He was there, and he always did a great job. He never let me down. We made a great case and put a lot of drug-dealing money launderers in jail. More than fifteen years have passed since we worked that case. Pete and I have lost touch over the years, but I have not forgotten all that he did; he was a true partner. That is how I will remember him. How he chose to run his personal life was his decision; I had no business judging it. As we discussed earlier, I was not the morality police.

Often times, during my FBI career, at some conference or training program, a self-proclaimed morality cop would pontificate, "If you can't respect the vows of your marriage, how can I expect you to live up to the commitments of this job?" On the surface, that sounded logical. In law enforcement, extra-marital affairs ran rampant. In my experiences, I never saw a direct correlation between marital indiscretions and job performance. While we may want to find fault with behavior that we do not approve of, we must rely on facts and specific knowledge. We cannot assume or rush to judgment – whether we like the final message or not.

My partner Carl, from my police days, and I would sometimes spend days off training together. We would work out and practice takedown and arrest techniques. Although there was no gun control in Virginia, we did not run into guns often. The folks there did like to fight. We could count on a good "duking it out" at least once a week. Staying in good shape was certainly in our best interests.

One night I pulled over a drunk driver who would not get out of his car. If a small, weak person takes a tight hold of a steering wheel, it is still hard to get him out of the car, even if you are significantly bigger and stronger. The driver I pulled over was fit and tough with tattoos on his bulging biceps. At this point in my career, I knew to call for backup. Carl, of course, was there in no time. We tugged on him a few times, and nothing happened. Then we looked at each other and realized that we were not using any of the training that we had practiced. Carl took out his kuboton, a small, round, hard plastic device applied to pressure points to force compliance. I then used a procedure whereby I attacked his head by pushing his jaw in one direction and pulling from under the neck in the other direction. It worked.

Actually, it worked too well. This two-hundred-pound gorilla went flying through the driver side window. We were not expecting that. All three of us went flying backwards. As we were beginning to fall, my instinct kicked in, and I turned him around so he would not fall on top of me, a bad position to be in. He turned completely around, and when he fell, he hit his face on the ground and I was on top. His nose started to bleed from the impact of the fall. We started struggling to get his hands behind his back to handcuff him.

At that point, a small crowd leaving a restaurant, and who had probably been drinking, came over to see what the fuss was. They saw two cops on top of one man with a bloody face. Did they jump to conclusions? Absolutely.

They started screaming brutality, and the crowd began to grow and get hostile. We called for more backup ASAP, and they responded quickly to handle the crowd while Carl and I finished the arrest. We quickly got the prisoner into my cruiser, and I took off.

My sergeant then started interviewing those who were claiming they witnessed police brutality. My sergeant asked for specifics of what they saw. Well, nobody saw what started the incident. Nobody saw the man initially resist arrest. Nobody saw what happened that led up to the bloody nose. Nobody saw either Carl or me hit the man or even verbally abuse him. All they saw was blood and jumped to conclusions. Soon the crowd began to realize that they had no complaint at all, and the matter just went away. People were certainly quick to judge and draw conclusions without having any of the facts.

I have found that the general public is usually quick to judge when there is a police shooting. Circumstances surrounding a shooting are rarely clear. Many times, the victim of the shooting appears to have been powerless against armed, trained police officers. Police are often criticized when several officers are on the scene, and they all shoot, resulting in a large number of rounds fired. This gives the appearance of "overkill," or what has been termed "contagious shooting." As of this writing, such an incident has recently occurred in New York City and is receiving much publicity. There are many explanations offered for this type of action.

Like most law enforcement officers, I have never fired my weapon at anybody and, accordingly, have not been involved in contagious shooting. I neither justify nor condemn these actions, having not personally experienced it. I have drawn my weapon many times and found myself in that scary position of just not knowing if I would have to pull that trigger. Let me offer some observations. Police shoot until the threat is eliminated. The number of rounds fired may not reflect the appropriateness or necessity of the shooting. If many rounds missed or failed to stop the assailant, naturally, more rounds will be fired. If several police officers are on the scene, they cannot stop and coordinate their shooting—first you, then me... That would not only be absurd, but deadly.

Each officer responds viscerally to perceived danger. His perception of danger is based on all the facts and circumstances present at the moment. And yes, another police officer firing his weapon is going to raise that officer's sense of imminent danger. One can argue that if the initial officer firing his weapon was wrong in his judgment to fire, then each police officer who fired was also wrong. Each police officer must be judged on his individual actions and on whether his perception of danger and his reaction to it were reasonable. But reasonable in whose eyes? That standard of reasonableness must be based on that of a trained, experienced police officer, not someone who does not have the training or the experience to understand the situation the police officer was in. I would not want to judge the medical decisions an emergency room doctor makes in moments of crisis; I have neither the training nor experience to make that judgment.

In the FBI, all field offices have a Citizens' Academy. This a great public service whereby citizens of high standing in the community attend classes one night a week for six to eight weeks at their local FBI office. They are given presentations on all the programs and violations worked by the FBI, such as terrorism, violent crime, cyber crime, and white-collar crime. The FBI does not share classified information with these citizens—though they often think they are getting some inside scoop—but they get a very personal briefing and time to get to know some of the agents.

I had the pleasure of initiating the Citizens' Academy in my community when I reported as SAC of the Minneapolis office. All of these Citizens' Academies throughout the country have been tremendous successes. My favorite class, the one we save for the last night, was the Shoot, Don't Shoot Scenarios. In these classes, we used virtual reality with technology circa 1980. The citizen was given a "gun" that fired infrared-type beams at a large screen. On the screen, an arrest scenario was played out, and the citizen was part of the scene, acting in the role of an FBI agent. The citizen could call out an order such as "Let's see your hands," and the operator of the machine could change the way the scenario unfolded. The scenes ranged from a hostage situation to armed fleeing felons to unarmed karate experts. These classes generated much discussion and debate, besides being fun. Most of the participants got themselves or their partner "killed" because they failed to shoot when they should have.

One of the most important lessons they learned was that even if there was a tragic mistake, the agent or police officer may have still acted appropriately. Let me explain. An officer responds to a suspicious circumstance one night. The area is not well lit. The suspicious individual does not respond to the officer's directions to "freeze." He then reaches into his jacket and pulls out his hand holding something in it. It looks like a gun. The officer shoots. It is not a gun. The person was a deaf mute and had pulled out a notepad and pen. An innocent man is shot dead by a cop.

Certainly, the tragic shooting of an unarmed, disabled individual would stir emotions and calls of a trigger-happy cop. On another occasion, the scenario is a little different. The person still does not respond to the officer and pulls something out of his jacket. This time, the officer waits until he can see exactly what is in the person's hand, so there is no mistake. Much better police work, right? The officer is shot dead.

Once again, we must apply the standard of reasonableness in the eyes of a trained, experienced officer. Officers are not required to allow someone to shoot at them before defending themselves. They are paid to take risks, but not suicidal ones. They are allowed and expected to protect themselves and make it home to their families. Sometimes, there will be a tragic mistake, yet the officer responded correctly. That is a hard concept to accept, but true.

After the citizens go through this training, they always talk about their changed perceptions. Weeks after one Citizens' Academy, I received a letter from one of our attendees. She not only thanked me for the opportunity but discussed the impact the Shoot, Don't Shoot Scenarios had on her perspective of police work. She could not believe that now she understood why a police officer could be justified shooting someone in the back as he was fleeing. She saw that in a scenario where the "bad guy" was running away. As it turned out, he was not simply running away; he was running for cover, or what we call a "tactical advantage," so he had a better shot at the cop while protecting himself. Did the officer have a right to prevent that? He most certainly did. Irrespective of whether the shooting was justified or not, as we know, a cop shooting someone in the back will never play fairly in the media.

Moving away from tragedy, there was one humorous example of being judgmental I think I will always remember. It occurred while I was working on the FBI NYPD Drug Task Force in New York. Our undercover agent, whom I will call Roberto, was on his way to an undercover meet, where a drug dealer was going to give Roberto drug money for Roberto to launder. Roberto was a legendary undercover agent in the FBI. His physical appearance was such that nobody ever suspected him of being "the man."

Waiting for Roberto to arrive at the restaurant, some of the cops planted themselves in the bar next door to keep watch. A few minutes after they sat down, someone robbed the bar. The cops took off in hot pursuit. A few of the agents and I heard the cops call it in on the radio. We all pulled our cars over and, with guns and radios in hand, ran into the streets to find our partners and help them. That kind of police activity caused quite a stir on those city blocks. In the meantime, Roberto was driving to his deal in an undercover vehicle, which had no radio. Roberto continued to follow the plan, got to the restaurant, and sat down with the drug dealer. The drug dealer told Roberto about the idiots who tried to rob the bar next door in front of a bunch of cops. He laughed about them as he handed over several hundred thousand dollars of drug money to an undercover FBI agent while under surveillance and being filmed. So much for rushing to judgment of a fellow felon. Our hapless drug dealer did not get the last laugh.

Judging is easy. When was the last time you were given the responsibilities of a police officer and were confronted with a life-and-death situation that required a decision and action in nanoseconds? Taking time to reflect in retrospect as to what you would have done is neither a fair nor a reliable method to judge such actions.

How does this apply to your daily business dealings? When I was studying accounting, my class was presented with a financial problem. Briefly, a company spent $100,000 on machinery that will save $50,000 a year, for at least the next five years, for a savings of $150,000 after deducting the cost of the machinery. The next year, there is a newer and improved model that will save the company $50,000 a year for the next ten years at a purchase price of 300,000 for a net savings of $200,000. Should they make the purchase?

Most of us decided no; when we added on the cost of the original $100,000 purchase, savings were reduced to $100,000, which was less than the original $150,000 savings. That seemed simple enough. However, without considering every possibility, our decision was wrong; we should not have counted the original expense of $100,000. That was a sunk cost, the money was spent; it was gone and should not affect future decisions. Making a decision for the future based on a past expense is known as the sunk cost bias. The sunk cost bias is related to the sciences of heuristics defined by Wikipedia as "…an adjective for experience-based techniques that help in problem solving, learning and discovery. Heuristic methods are used to rapidly come to a solution that is hoped to be close to the best possible answer, or 'optimal solution'. Heuristics are 'rules of thumb', educated guesses, intuitive judgments or simply common sense."

Related to heuristics is Prospect Theory, defined by Wikipedia as, "…a theory that describes decisions between alternatives that involve risk, i.e. alternatives with uncertain outcomes, where the probabilities are known. The model is descriptive: it tries to model real-life choices, rather than optimal decisions." Prospect Theory was developed by psychologists Daniel Kahneman and Amos Tversky. In the simplest terms I can offer, as well as understand, Kahneman and Tversky identified certain "cognitive biases" which lead to errors in our judgment and decisions. The sunk cost bias is one example. We give value to the sunk cost as we do not want to face that we may have made a decision that did not have the desired outcome. Look at this from the personal perspective. You bought tickets to a concert. On the night of the concert, you are offered to attend a different social function, which you would prefer over the concert. How many of us would choose the concert? We do not want to think that we wasted money, as if not knowing a better offer was coming, was some sort of failure. We should accept the new and better offer; the money for the tickets is sunk; it is gone. Going or not going to the concert will not affect that. Yet, we will most likely go to the concert, the less desirable option.

Another cognitive bias is the confirmation bias, which is a tendency to place more weight on evidence or other indicators that support what we already believe. Commonly cited as an example of confirmation bias is a tendency of researchers to structure their methodology and testing in a manner that will support their beliefs. The status quo bias causes us to prefer no change. Does that sound familiar, perhaps like the threat of, "We've always done it that way." There is also the bandwagon bias, which is a tendency to follow the common actions or thoughts of several others. Does this remind you of the threat of Groupthink or the mob mentality? Poor business decisions can result from these potential flaws in our thought processes. Understanding these biases gives us reason to pause, to stop and think, and determine if our judgment is based on a firm understanding of the facts or clouded by what we want to hear.

Do not be quick to judge based on appearance, rumor, or limited facts. What you heard is probably not correct. Remember, you were not there. Learn the full scope of the circumstances, get the full story, understand the other person's perspective and biases, and then decide. Using your judgment and being judgmental are two different things.

In business, we must be careful not to allow these biases to affect our decisions; we must analyze our options based on verifiable facts. To make decisions, especially involving personnel, which are not based on facts that can be substantiated is inviting liability exposure. Focus on learning from the past, not reliving it, for the past is a sunk cost. Today, we are faced with handling multiple challenges simultaneously and making decisions within a short timeframe. You must learn to…

CHAPTER 16

Lesson: <u>Multitask</u>
Or, "I must do this, that, and the other thing,
which are all priorities. You do this, that, and
that other thing. Let's regroup in an hour
and see where we are."

One time, I walked into my supervisor's office to ask for assistance on an arrest plan I was putting together. I was on the drug squad, and this supervisor I will call Chris. Chris snapped at me and said, "Tabman, whatta you expect? I can only handle one thing at a time." That struck me. We were a thirty-man drug task force in Queens, New York. There were a lot of things happening at any given moment. Time was not always on our side. Should the supervisor be able to handle only one matter at a time?

During my training period as a police officer, I was sitting in the cruiser with one of the cops on my squad whom I'll call Rick. Rick was sipping his coffee, filling out an accident report, and answering questions from a citizen all at once. I was trying to pay attention to what he was doing. All of a sudden, he picked up the radio and said, "Ten-four." Through all those distractions, he was still able to monitor the radio and respond to a call for service. He quickly put his paperwork away, politely excused himself from his conversation with the citizen, and took off for the call. He remembered the address broadcast over the radio without writing it down. I had not even heard the radio call. How did he do so many things at once? Would I ever learn to do that? It seemed like such a valuable, if not vital, skill to acquire.

A very basic function of a patrol officer was handling traffic accidents. As I have already stated, I hated those. Traffic accidents were true multitasking assignments. The officer had to conduct an on-the-spot investigation to determine fault; redirect traffic; record license, registration, and insurance information; take conflicting statements from the irate motorists; find witnesses; write tickets; issue subpoenas; and then write a report. I was concerned that my dislike of these calls was due to the multitasking nature of them and that I would never develop those skills I so admired.

One night, I had a citizen accompany me on the ride-along program during the 4 p.m. through midnight shift. That was usually the best shift. Until about 6:30 p.m., most of the calls were traffic related. After that, as night set in, the more exciting police calls of robberies and burglaries occurred. As I was patrolling, out of the corner of my eye, I observed what I considered a suspicious vehicle parked at the end of a school parking lot. I called it in on the radio, pulled over, checked out the driver, and found it to be nothing. I moved on and forgot all about it—just another routine task. A few minutes later, my ride-along said something that surprised me.

"I can't believe you were able to do that."

"Do what?" I asked, honestly not knowing what he was referring to.

"How you were able to drive, talk to me, listen to the radio, and see that car parked all the way down the block. It was suspicious, but I didn't even see it there. How did you do so many things at once?"

Trying to hide my spontaneous smile, I instantly realized that I had finally arrived. Never noticing it, but just from experience, I had developed those multitasking skills so necessary to being a successful, and alive, police officer. What else did I learn? I learned that I just did not like working traffic accidents.

In today's world of instant communication and data flow, you must be able to multitask. You must be able to process numerous streams of information, data, and demands for your attention. In our war on terrorism, it is not the lack of intelligence that threatens us, it is the plethora of intelligence that we must cull and analyze to find that one tidbit of actionable intelligence that will thwart a terrorist attack. In both the public and private sectors, we must learn to deal with information overload. In 2009, high unemployment rates highlight that those fortunate to have a job will have to absorb the responsibilities of those who were not quite as fortunate. Completing these additional tasks, perhaps unrelated to your prime duties, requires multitasking.

Every person believes that his crisis or concerns are a priority and needs your undivided attention. Little things, like moving the work on your desk aside, shutting your office door, or holding telephone calls will convey your commitment to giving that person his due share of your attention. Those are small gestures that convey an important message. At the same time, you must do this cautiously, for if you continuously give too much time to something that is not a priority to the organization, and invite unnecessary distractions, performance will suffer. Prioritize. Draw the line on how much time you will spend on lower priority issues, but communicate that with tact and diplomacy. That, in and of itself, is multitasking. Multitasking must be approached with caution, however.

Studies have shown that multitasking may result in reduced productivity and an inefficient use of time. Many articles discussing multitasking reference a study entitled, *Executive Control of Cognitive Processes in Task Switching,* by Joshua S. Rubinstein, David E. Meyer and Jeffrey E. Evans, published in the *Journal of Experimental Psychology: Human Perspectives and Performance,* 2001, Vol. 27, No. 4, 763-797. The study found that we experience mental downtime when we switch tasks, referred to as switching-time costs. More time is lost when "...switching from unfamiliar tasks to familiar tasks than for switching in the opposite direction."

In an online (latimes.com) Los Angeles Times article, entitled, *We're all multitasking, but what's the cost?* author Melissa Healy discusses the dangers of multitasking. Noting that our ability to multitask originates in our brain's frontal cortex, Healy states, "The same region of the brain is where we pull off another uniquely human trick that is key to multitasking: 'marking' the spot at which a task has been interrupted, so we can return to it later." According to Healy, Dr. Jordan Grafman, a neuropsychologist, points out that the frontal cortex is "…the part of the human brain that is most damaged as a result of prolonged stress…The kind of stress…you might feel when overwhelmed by the demands of multitasking." Healy quotes psychiatrist Edward Hallowell describing multitaskers as, "…impulsive, curt, abrasive, no lead-in, no small talk, no body language." I can understand that. As a self-proclaimed multitasker, I often learned that I had been perceived in those terms when I had no intention or desire of coming off that way. Now I understand why.

In July 2009, the New York Times obtained a report by the United States Department of Transportation, National Highway Traffic Safety Administration, entitled, *Status Summary: Using Wireless Communication Devices While Driving, Last Updated: July 2003*. What made news about this report was that it was withheld out of fear that reporting the dangers of cell phone use while driving would anger Congress. Whether that is true, and the reasons and the politics behind it are not the issue for this book. The findings, however, are germane. The report notes:

- "…general delay in information processing and degradation of driver performance…equivalent for hand-held and hands-free cell phone users."
- "…a difficult conversation may have an adverse effect of driving…"

- "…changes in driving behavior…due to increases in cognitive demands associated with mobile phone usage, including hands-free phones."
- "…increases in cognitive demand due to listening to complex messages via hands-free phone results in degraded driving performance…"

Nobody would argue that cell phone usage during driving is dangerous. This study strongly suggests that even hands-free telephone conversations are dangerous. Multiple, simultaneous demands on our senses present a risk to our mental acuity and physical response times.

President Obama has, at times, been criticized for attacking too many issues at once. The President has been clear that each issue requires immediate attention. His focus on multiple issues has led others to recognize him as a president of our times, having the ability to multitask. The need to multitask in today's fluid and highly stimulus-rich work environment does not appear to be abating, but growing.

There are methods for reducing the risks of multitasking. Tasks that do not require a significant amount of creative thought — can be completed on "autopilot" — are good candidates for multitasking. Tasks that affect different areas of physical stimuli may be addressed simultaneously. Move from the complex to the more simple, not the opposite, to reduce the mental "down time" of multitasking. Recognize which activities require your undivided attention.

Have a plan for handling your in-box. Learn how to quickly scan long documents to pick up the pertinent points, a type of speed-reading for business. Once again, prioritize your paperwork. If some lower priority work can be knocked out in a matter of moments, it might be worth addressing that first, just to get rid of it. Know what you need to know and let someone else worry about the things that you do not need to know. Delegate. As an executive, you generally do not need to know the specifics of each matter, but see the big picture. There are times, such as during a crisis, when you will need to see the forest and the trees. While some of these research studies suggest that multitasking cannot be learned, my personal experience as a police officer suggests otherwise.

A significant aspect of multitasking is sharing information and delegating responsibility. Often that cannot be achieved without...

CHAPTER 17

Lesson: <u>The Dreaded Meeting</u>
Or, "When is this over?"

Nobody likes meetings. We all complain about them. Yet, meetings persist; they seem to be a necessary evil. In today's world of e-mail, videoconferencing, text messaging, and all sorts of advanced communication systems, the meeting has taken on a new face. With so many ways to disseminate information to so many people instantaneously, meetings should be shorter and less frequent. I did not see that in the FBI; we had a lot of long, long meetings. Most of those meetings were of questionable necessity. I found that a meeting should not last more than one hour. That was somewhat arbitrary, but I always got the feeling that the attention span had a precipitous decline after one hour, a point of diminishing returns. That of course, could be my limited attention span.

What is the purpose of the meeting? Is there an objective? Sometimes, those questions cannot be answered; or the answer is clearly "no." Many meetings are regularly scheduled, such as for every other Tuesday, and the meetings are held whether they are needed or not. Justification is usually to "touch base" or "just to get a feel of what is going on." These are valid reasons. These reasons, however, must be weighed against the time and productivity that is lost during the meeting

The most common meeting in police work was the roll call. Every day, before hitting the streets, you knew to be in roll call, and on time. These meetings had a definite purpose. First, as defined by its name, we had to know who was showing up to work. Unlike other businesses, someone's absence for even one day required a shifting of responsibilities. No patrol sector could be left without coverage. The officers and the dispatchers had to know who was responsible for what sectors for each and every shift, 24/7. The second major purpose was to share corporate information such as policy changes, cases that may spark media requests, crime trends throughout the county or tactical information such as or where plainclothes detectives may be on a stakeout. Time was allotted for training.

Roll calls were usually lighthearted, with a certain amount of locker-room-type banter going around for a few laughs. Because another squad was still on the streets waiting for you to get out there so they could end their shift, the length of the roll call was predetermined. I actually enjoyed roll call and found it to be a great way to start what could prove to be a very intense workday.

Business meetings modeled after roll calls could prove to be very effective: its purpose was clear; important information was shared; tension was reduced by an informal atmosphere; there was team interaction; and because it had limited time, distractions had to be kept to a minimum. I have heard about some police departments that hold very military-like roll calls. Officers standing at attention, barked at by their superior officers. Having not experienced that, I cannot pass judgment, but I like the model I experienced in Fairfax County; I think it worked.

The FBI did not have roll calls. Maybe we should have. In the FBI, meetings were not quite as efficient. Maybe egos were just bigger, but it seemed that so many people loved to hear themselves talk. Many meetings did not appear driven by a specific purpose or agenda; they were scheduled and something, or anything had to be discussed ad nauseum. Calling meetings just to be able to say you meet with your people regularly is not a responsible use of precious time. If there is enough information to warrant scheduled meetings, such as every Tuesday, fine. If you are not disseminating or taking in important information, you should rethink that schedule. As in roll calls, a certain amount of joking and exchange of friendly ribbing should be expected in a meeting of personnel who know each other and work together on a regular basis. If allowed to go on too long, you are wasting time, and those who do not wish to partake in such banter will resent being forced to sit through it.

In the book *Ruthless Execution: What Business Leaders Do When Their Companies Hit the Wall*, author Amir Hartman describes some of the tactics Lou Gerstner used to turn around IBM. Hartman points out that Gerstner "…cut meetings short and expressed annoyance at anyone who wasted time. He outlawed…prepared slides and overhead projector presentations…"

Do you need everyone there the whole time? When I was the SAC, a supervisory staff meeting included agent supervisors and support supervisors. Customarily, all would sit through the entire meeting. I noticed that the support personnel did not seem particularly interested in the briefings by the agent supervisors. I did not view that as a lack of loyalty or not having interest in the work of the whole office, but they had things to do and what was being discussed did not directly affect them. Conversely, what the support supervisors had to say did affect the agents, especially matters such as computer problems. There was an easy solution. I had the support people give their presentations first. The rest of the staff and I would address any significant issues with them. Then, they were free to leave. They were also invited to stay and hear what was happening on the agent side of the house, if they wished. Once in a while, someone did stay, but usually, you were blown out of your seat by the strong wind created as they rushed out of the room.

While Lou Gerstner was turning IBM around, Sam Palmisano, who would eventually succeed Gerstner as IBM CEO, took a number of steps to improve productivity while he was head of IBM's PC Division. According to Hartman in *Ruthless Execution*, Palmisano directed employees "…to attend only those meetings that were vital to their work…" The effective management of meetings is an integral element of efficient business operations.

One of the most unusual meetings I had was when I was an inspector in charge for the FBI. About halfway through an inspection, each team would present to me the issues that they had identified and what route they were planning to take. This meeting was called "crunch." The teams were anywhere from three or four people to more than a dozen, and the number of teams could range from ten to over twenty depending on the size of the office. Crunch was an all-day affair, and in the larger offices, it could last for two days. It was very intense. I relied heavily on crunch. Even though I was being fed information the whole week prior to crunch through the chain of command, this gave me a chance to hear it firsthand from the agents actually doing the groundwork and to personally observe and evaluate them.

Not only was the actual information important, but the demeanor of the agent and the nature of his presentation was key for me. I would assess the thoroughness of the agent's work and determine whether he really understood the issues, and at times, look for signs that an agent was starting to "Stockholm." This term was a reference to the Stockholm syndrome. The Stockholm syndrome was one of the first lessons you learned in Hostage Negotiation School. This is a phenomenon whereby hostages may start to identify with and become sympathetic to their captors, so much so that they themselves become a threat to law enforcement, even during a rescue attempt. That is one reason why police will have all people held hostage leave the area with their hands up and may even handcuff everybody until the situation is completely under control. From the outside looking in, it seems like harsh treatment of a hostage, but it is necessary.

So, how does the Stockholm syndrome relate to inspections and crunch? Sometimes an inspector in charge would notice that there was an issue arising relative to the performance of a particular agent in the field office under inspection, but the inspecting agent seemed reluctant to address it. That came from the feeling of connection to the other agent—"That could be me" or "I don't want to hurt a brother agent." This did not happen often, but it happened often enough to be alert for it.

Crunch had a legendary reputation for being high stress and a place where agents "crashed and burned" because they were unprepared for the questions posed by the inspector in- charge. This was viewed as not only embarrassing but potentially career damaging.

I remember my first inspection, not as the inspector in charge but as one of the staff. The inspector in charge, whom I'll call Gus, had a reputation for being brutal, tough on the office he was inspecting and just as tough on his staff. One night, early in the inspection, Gus stopped by and had a drink with a few of us. I did not get the impression that his reputation was truly reflective of him. A few days later, we had crunch, and I gave my oral presentation. When I blurted out a certain statistic regarding arrests, Gus questioned it, as it did not sound right. I fumbled through my paperwork and could not find any other information, so I asserted that my numbers were correct. Gus let it go, but he clearly was not convinced. I kept looking through my papers and found that I had quoted the wrong number and I was way off, explaining Gus's reaction. In my mind, I debated letting it go or admitting to my mistake. In a few minutes, there was a break in the action. I spoke up.

"Excuse me, sir, but it seems I have suffered from a great case of crunchitis, and I gave you the wrong number." There was silence. Gus looked at me.

"Crunch-itis?" he repeated and then paused. "Crunchitis, that's funny." Then he burst out laughing.

Now everyone was laughing, perhaps the result of Groupthink. After that, Gus and I got along very well, and he invited me on all his inspections. Sometimes a little humor can go a long way. Humor can be a dangerous path. We all have very different ideas of what constitutes funny.

After I became an inspector in charge, I tried to keep my crunches "light," allowing a little humor to be interjected but not enough to prolong an already long meeting. Sticking only to the important issues and not allowing ourselves to get sidetracked by extraneous data, we got through the crunch with a clear understanding of where we were heading. If I wasn't comfortable with answers I was getting or suspected poor performance from any of my staff, I would allow their presentation to conclude and then would address my concerns through my supervisory staff. I never embarrassed anybody, raised my voice, or began to criticize. That does not mean I didn't ask probing questions or give suggestions or directions of further things to do, but I tried to avoid sending someone into a crash-and-burn mode. That would be unprofessional and unnecessary. It would also hurt the efficacy of the inspection. With that worry on their minds, staff performance would not have been optimal. I tried to avoid any more instances of crunchitis. I cannot imagine that embarrassing anybody during a meeting would have had a positive outcome. I found crunches to be one of the very few meetings I considered necessary, valuable and effective irrespective of the time required.

To be effective and efficient, meetings must adhere to rules and standards, like any other business process. Meetings must start exactly on time. If someone is late, he must experience the uncomfortable feeling of walking into the room while the meeting is in progress. Everyone must be given ample opportunity to speak their mind. If you are leading a meeting, you must be cognizant of those who would tend to dominate and try to intimidate others from disagreeing. You must protect and encourage those who are afraid of criticism of their comments or ideas. If someone is continually critical of others, ask him to offer a better solution. Encourage honest and fair debate. Have an agenda. It need not be written down, but there should be a definite purpose to the meeting. Even if you are just seeking updates, that is information sharing, and that is the agenda. Use meetings to disseminate information that cannot be more effectively and efficiently shared through emails. Yet, do not use emails to avoid face-to-face meetings that are necessary for personal, sensitive or confrontational matters.

Keep one thing in mind— the meeting must end. I had one supervisor who seemed like he just did not want the meetings to end. At what appeared to be the logical conclusion of the meeting, he would ask if there were any questions or anything else. The room would remain silent. He would then address each person individually and ask if he had anything to discuss. The answers still would be "no." Then, he would bring up some random issue and ask the person involved to talk about it. If the person really had wanted to discuss that issue there and then, he had ample opportunity to do so. The meeting was over; the supervisor just did not want to stop.

Start your meeting on time. Have an agenda and stick to it. Minimize distractions. Allow ample time for questions and discussion, assuring that the questions and discussions are germane to the issues at hand; do not become sidetracked. Assure an environment that encourages participation, but do not allow anyone to dominate the time or intimidate others. Know when the meeting is over and end it! Approach meetings as all other business processes and maintain strong...

CHAPTER 18

Lesson: <u>Internal Controls</u>
Or, "That's not just for financial reporting."

One time, as the SAC, I was asked to give a speech on leadership to a group of police executives who were graduating from an FBI-sponsored police leadership school. I had many canned speeches ready to go, but thought that this event warranted something more original. As well, several officers in the audience had already heard me speak. I did not want someone to hear something from me that he had already heard. I knew I had to try something different. During classes that I had taken to prepare for my CPA exam, I learned about a concept called internal controls. Despite being an accounting principal, which suggests boredom by its very nature, I found the concept rather interesting. Then again, I became a CPA; maybe my sense of interesting was not a good barometer for gauging the interest of my audience. How would a group of experienced, probably somewhat jaded police executives, enjoying their graduation dinner, appreciate a speech that was based on accounting principles? I could not imagine, but I took the risk, prepared a speech about internal control concepts and tied it to police work.

First, I reminded them that I was a former police officer. That was my way of connecting with my audience. Then I told them how I spent most of my career in New York City working with NYPD detectives investigating organized crime and drugs. What was the message I was trying to convey? I was trying to tell them that I was not a typical CPA, and that actually, I was kind of a cool guy. I doubt they bought off on that message, but they listened courteously, and the speech appeared to be a success. I measure success of a speech by the number of people who come up to me afterwards to either thank me or ask some more questions.

Internal controls were designed by the Committee of Sponsoring Organizations of the Treadway Commission. Known as COSO, the committee defined internal controls as a group of managerial principles that consist of five major components with seventeen subcomponents. The primary goal of internal controls, especially in view of the financial crisis, is to assure that financial statements are free of any material misstatements. Another goal of internal controls is effective and efficient operations and compliance with applicable laws and regulations. Let's look at the five major concepts of internal controls and how we have already shown them to be important not only in the life of a law enforcement officer but in business.

The first internal control is the control environment. The control environment sets the managerial tone and lays the foundation for the organization. Management's style and philosophy as well as the ethical values of the organization are encompassed in this first factor. Management sets the tone by their words and actions. For example, we discussed how the handling of evidence was an extremely important step in criminal investigations, and successful prosecutions often rested on the proper handling of evidence. By taking personal ownership of items from the Oklahoma City bombing and then again from ground zero at the World Trade Center, what message was the FBI sending to its employees? First, did it set an environment for questionable handling of evidence? Had the FBI addressed this at Oklahoma City, it would not have arisen as an issue after 9/11. Secondly, I cannot imagine I was the only employee to express concern over this practice. Did the FBI set an environment whereby employees felt uncomfortable, if not afraid, of questioning policy? We also discussed the outrageous conduct of Dennis Kozlowski of Tyco. At that party, did anybody consider that Tyco's control environment was out of control?

Are you aware of the control environment of your organization? Do you know what tone is being set and how your messages are perceived? Do employees feel free to report fraud, waste, misconduct or questionable business practices? How do you know? Do you look and listen?

The next internal control is risk assessment. We spent considerable time on managing risk and crisis management. I have pointed out that the FBI had numerous "administrative"

risks besides the inherent risks of law enforcement activities. For example, the handling of informants was high risk.
Therefore, additional safeguards were required in addition
to the informant file reviews. As we discussed earlier, immediately following 9/11, many businesses asked me what they
could do to improve security. When I asked how they wanted
to improve security and what they were trying to protect
against, they could not answer. If they wanted to protect
against a 9/11-type attack, they were being unrealistic. What
were the real threats? Suicide bombers? Anthrax lettrs? Are
there realistic ways to protect against these threats that will
allow your business to continue in a normal and profitable
fashion? Is a security guard looking at driver licenses really
going to reduce the risk? You must also weigh the cost and
impact on customers, personnel and logistics against the
likeliness of a particular attack. As we know, there are many
other risks besides these physical ones. Economic, business,
and environmental factors pose risks. Have you identified
the relevant risks to your business? Are the risks primarily
internal or external? You must identify and assess the realistic threats and take appropriate countermeasures. Assess
and plan.

Following risk assessment are control activities, which
are defined as your policies and procedures to assure your
business operations are carried out the way you expect
them to be carried out. For example, in the FBI, when handling valuable or drug evidence, two agents were supposed

to process the evidence together and witness for each other the counting of money, weighing of drugs, and sealing of the evidence all the way through its submission to the evidence vault. This was a valuable control activity that reduced the risk of mishandling or losing evidence or even an accusation of improper activities by the agents. Also included in these control activities are approvals levels and processes, reconciliations, and performance reviews.

I vividly remember one occasion in New York when I was on the drug task force unsealing evidence to return to the arrestee's attorney. The evidence was an envelope containing $100 — in low denomination bills — that I had taken from this prisoner at the time of the arrest. At my desk in my office, with most of the squad sitting around, I did this by myself. As I counted the money out for the return, I counted only $80. Counting two more times led to the same results. I went into a minor panic. Would I be accused of stealing $20? It was such a small amount of money compared to the money we seized from drug dealers that I did not think of having a second agent with me just to return it, which was proper protocol. At that moment, I realized I had made a big mistake. I should have followed the procedure to the letter. That was an internal control, and it clearly served a purpose. After another count, I did finally find the other twenty folded up in the small wad of cash and I breathed a big sigh of relief. Not realizing another agent from across the room had been watching me and enjoying the panic on my face, I heard, "Glad you found that money, hey, Tabman," he called across the room with a laugh. At that moment, I was able to share the laugh with him.

Do your employees handle sensitive data, trade secrets, intellectual property, or confidential client information? Is there sensitive data just waiting to be plucked off your network? Do you have policies and procedures in place to reduce the chance of mishandling or misappropriating such information? Are these policies and procedures enforced? With today's concerns over identity theft, think of how many high-profile losses of personal data have been reported in the media. The costs involved in actual losses, making proper notifications, assessing and fixing the vulnerability and potential damage to your reputation can be staggering.

The fourth component of the framework is information and communication. We have discussed the importance of clear communications. Internal and external events and all information necessary to assure optimal performance must be communicated throughout the organization; employees must have access to all pertinent information that will empower them to do their jobs. This may not be the best example, but I remember my attempt to stay informed of world events during my first tour as a supervisor at FBI headquarters in the mid 1990s. I was in a pod in the center of this huge building. There was no radio reception and this was before continuous cable news in the office was an accepted practice. The first thing I did in the morning was to read the newspaper. I read only the news—no comics, no crossword puzzles, and not even the sports. Just the news. As an FBI agent, I found that remaining informed of current events was quite important. My boss, however, had an inexplicable rule about reading the newspaper at your desk. I never figured out why, but she simply would not tolerate anybody reading the newspaper at the desk. Many of my friends and associates outside the FBI were lawyers and businessmen, and generally well-educated people who would call me to discuss current issues, crises and events, especially involving the FBI. Those times when I did not know what they were talking about, I felt ridiculous. In my attempt to be compliant with my boss' directive, I waited until I took a coffee break in the cafeteria and read my newspaper there. She chastised me for that too. Why would reading the newspaper be taboo? I could not figure that one out.

When I first became a supervisor in a field office, I encouraged my agents to read the newspaper and stay informed. I enjoyed intellectual discourse among the squad that some of the news stories inspired. While I did not want them to discuss "Dear Abby," I did encourage them to read the sports page. Why? Even though I was not a sports fan myself, the fact was that many people enjoyed discussing sports. We were in the people business. We needed to make friends, develop informants, and get people to cooperate. The more things in common you have to talk about, the greater the chances of developing a congenial and cooperative relationship. It was all a matter of having, and getting information.

The fifth internal control is monitoring. That is almost self-explanatory. I remember one very keen example of the FBI's failure to monitor its own internal controls. In one office where I was a member of management, we were conducting a routine inventory of evidence. This was a very important control activity. During the audit, we found that a large amount of marijuana, seized as drug evidence, could not be accounted for. Missing drug evidence is not a good thing, to put it mildly. The marijuana had been packaged up years earlier and shipped to the DEA lab in Washington, D.C. for analysis. Yes, it was shipped; the FBI did not personally deliver all evidence to the lab. All the available shipping controls were put on the package so it could be tracked, including a return receipt. A receipt was never returned. As so much time had passed, the shipment could not be traced nor could the status of the receipt be determined. Where were the drugs? Nobody could say for sure. The case did not go to court, so the evidence was never asked for by the case agent, and that agent had already transferred to another office.

So, who was aware that the drugs were unaccounted for? Surprisingly, nobody. We did not monitor our own internal controls, which created not only a potential risk to a prosecution but opened the door for serious accusations. We did have to report the matter to our Office of Professional Responsibility for investigation. There should have been some internal control to alert the office when no receipt was returned. We quickly implemented a simple, automated procedure to monitor the delivery of mail and notify us if a receipt was not returned.

Monitoring is not for processes only. Did the FBI properly monitor the relationship between the male agent and the female Chinese spy? My guess would be no. Also, the failure to monitor led to the FBI's high rate of noncompliance with the laws surrounding National Security Letters.

Assure that your internal controls are in place, utilized, and subject to monitoring and periodic review. Think of monitoring as an internal control for your internal controls. Internal controls should not be a theory or separate aspect of your operation; they should coalesce with your daily operating activities.

Another consideration for many businesses is that internal controls have become important in assuring compliance with the Sarbanes-Oxley Act. Rules and procedures must be established and implemented for a particular, identifiable purpose. Many times, policies and procedures are outdated due to technology or changes in the law. Internal controls must add value to your operations. To be effective, they must be enforced and periodically reevaluated to determine their efficacy and continued necessity. Internal controls are important, but nothing can replace basic...

CHAPTER 19

Lesson: Instinct
Or, "I just know."

When I was in the police academy, the police department psychologist came to speak to us. She gave an interesting presentation, discussing the instinct that we would develop as we matured as police officers. Could instinct be developed? By its very definition, it seemed that one had to be born with that ability to be considered instinct. Or, can it develop from training and experience? What kind of instinct would we develop? The psychologist assured us that we would learn how to know almost immediately when someone was lying; we would be able to quickly size up a situation, walk into a room, and determine the nature of relationships. Surprisingly, in her words, she also said that we would be able to get a quick read on people and immediately be able to identify the assholes. Is that instinct or is it just honed powers of observation? I believe that the depth of one's instinct is mostly innate but can be developed up to a certain point. There are police officers who do not have the instinct to detect the dangers and pitfalls that cops must detect. Most of them do not stay on the job long. Instinct has been mentioned several times already in discussing other characteristics and principles. It is an integral element of success. In this chapter, we'll take a look at some principles and examples of instinct.

Let's look at a question from the beginning of the book that we have not yet answered.

Why didn't Scout 36 Adam respond Code 3 (lights and siren) to the gang fight with chains and knives? I heard the call; it sounded like an emergency to me. I was still a rookie driving with another senior officer. I didn't want to sound like I was questioning his judgment, but I had to know why such a call did not receive a priority response. Politely, I asked, trying hard to make it sound like it was more for my own edification rather than questioning his actions. He gave a great answer. He had been on patrol for a long time. He could tell by the nature of the call and from where the complaint originated, that it was not worth rushing over. When we arrived on the scene, we found a few teenagers just hanging out. Maybe they were a little noisy, but they weren't causing any real trouble. This was far from being a gang fight with chains and knives. Scout 36 Adam just knew it. As with so many other skills that I observed in my fellow police officers, I wondered if I would develop that instinct and know things just because "I knew."

A year later, I was on patrol on my own, no longer the rookie on the squad. I got called to a domestic dispute, one of the most common calls for a patrol unit. Domestic disputes are, potentially, one of the most dangerous calls. At these disputes, emotions are running high and everybody is unpredictable. You can decide to arrest the husband, and then the wife, who has just been beaten, suddenly turns on you. Many police injuries are sustained in domestic disputes.

I arrived at the scene of this dispute and found the husband, a young man about thirty years old, outside the apartment complex with his father. I spoke with them, and they seemed very reasonable and clearly not looking for a confrontation with the wife, and certainly not with the police. The husband just wanted to get into the apartment and get some of his stuff. The wife was refusing. As I spoke with them, I got a call over the radio. The wife had called in to warn us that the husband was carrying a weapon. That call gave me every right to have him "assume the position" and pat him down. I did not, which brings us to the other question we have not yet answered.

Why would I risk my safety like that? I knew that this man was not armed; I could tell from the call that the wife was just trying to harass him through me. By the timing of the call, I realized that she was probably watching us from the window and tried to exploit an opportunity for her advantage. How did I know? I just knew. I was not going to be used like that. I did calmly direct him and his father to assure that they did not take their hands out of my sight and make any sudden gestures. I could still be cautious without subjecting anybody to public embarrassment. After I told them that, the husband asked me, "Did she say I had a gun?" When I replied yes, I could tell that he and his father were not surprised. My partner, Carl, pulled up a few minutes later to see if I needed help. He asked if I patted them down. I said yes and that everything was OK. I knew Carl very well and usually knew what he was thinking; he was one of the best cops in the department, and I knew that he would not have agreed with my decision.

Doing something contrary to Carl's instinct was risky. Let's look at an example of just how sharp Carl's instinct was. He was on patrol one night and stopped a car for a routine traffic violation. There was nothing extraordinary about the man he stopped but Carl kept him in conversation, just due to a gut feeling something may be wrong. While talking to him, Carl noticed that up the block, in a small neighboring town, the police were running Code 3. Carl took the initiative and asked the dispatcher to contact that police department to find out what they were running on. They were responding to a murder. Carl began to look around the car he stopped and started finding evidence of the crime. Carl made an arrest for murder, not something that routinely happens while out on patrol. Pure instinct.

One night when I responded to a dispute in a quiet neighborhood, there were already two other officers at the scene. They had just wrestled to the ground a teenager who was yelling incoherently and obviously had been out of control before I arrived. I talked to his friends, who said they had gone out to a bar in Georgetown (a barhopping part of D.C. at the time) and just did some drinking and hanging out. Neither they nor their friend had gotten drunk, but on the way home, their friend just started acting crazy. They seemed like nice kids and were credible. I wondered if their friend did not fall victim to having his drink spiked.

Soon, the young man calmed down. He promised to behave if the cops let him up. At that moment, something struck me. I knew that when the kid was let up, he would lash out. Somehow, with all the people in this crowd, I knew he would attack me. He got up. Almost immediately, he turned towards me and attacked, trying to punch me right in the face. Instantly, I got him down and handcuffed in seconds without getting hit or having to hurt the young man. I did not even remember doing it; it just came naturally. That was part of my training and experience. I was ready, because I knew it was going to happen. How did I know it was going to happen exactly the way it did? Just instinct.

Another time I went with my instinct was when I was a new supervisor taking over the drug squad. For a number of reasons, the squad had very low morale, and the two most senior agents, who greatly influenced the younger agents, insisted on whining, complaining, and generally making the squad a miserable place to be. Statistical accomplishments were low, almost nonexistent. That was an aberration for any drug squad; arrests usually came easily. I held a meeting with the squad in an attempt to get them more excited about their work. Sharing my experiences from working drug trafficking and money laundering for several years in New York City, I was hoping to inspire some creative thought and motivate them to approach their work with a new sense of enthusiasm. What I saw were glazed-over eyes and staring at the ceiling. There was one exception. A brand-new rookie agent was watching me and listening. She was even taking notes. She was actually interested in what I had to say. At that moment, I just knew that she was going to be my key to reviving this squad. Her demeanor told me that she was willing to give things a try. The big problem was that she was very attractive. I knew that any special attention I gave her was fodder for rumors. That is a risk in any office. I would be cautious and alert to that. High risk, high reward.

Shortly into her training period, I assigned her cases and gave her guidance and advice. She listened and tried. She quickly was finding success. She developed informants, started wiretaps, and began making some great cases. I rewarded her by assigning her one of the new cars (a status symbol for agents) and later a cash award. Her success did inspire the other agents to start working, and things began to turn around. Soon, the squad was making arrests and knocking off methamphetamine labs at an astonishing pace. We were so successful that my squad missed the office holiday party because we had to serve a warrant on another meth lab. As for the rumors, I never heard any, which only means I never heard about them, not that they didn't arise.

When discussing instinct, I would be remiss not to mention author Malcolm Gladwell's tremendously successful book *Blink*, which explored instinct and what he termed "The Theory of Thin Slices," which Gladwell described as the ability to make decisions with a minimal amount of

information. The book is replete with examples of successful and some not-so-successful examples of using one's instinct. One interesting subject of his studies was the actor
Tom Hanks. Gladwell relates how producer Brian Grazer
knew in an instant that Tom Hanks was the right person for
the movie *Splash*. This was in 1983, before Hanks was the
superstar he is today. Later, going against advice, Grazer
cast Hanks as an astronaut in the movie *Apollo 13*. The
question was whether Hanks would be believable as an
astronaut. Grazer's instinct saw something else. Gladwell
quoted Grazer's instinctive thoughts: "Who does America
want to save? Tom Hanks. We don't want to see him die.
We like him too much." I do not think there was much
question about that.

We often talk about people's instincts—to make
money, for example. Did they always have that ability, or
did it develop from experience? Either way, in business, as
in police work, while there is always a learning curve, aspects of the job must become instinctive at a certain point,
or that employee will not perform optimally. Whether it
is in negotiations, dealing with clients and subordinates, or
recognizing potential problems by reading a report, our
employees must be able to protect the interests of our organizations and take the right action by instinct.

Do all jobs require a certain amount of instinct to be
successful? Maybe not. Perhaps some are done by rote so
that no instinct is necessary, just knowledge of how to carry
out a particular task. Most levels of responsibility are not

that simple and do require a certain amount of instinct. At what point do you decide if your employee is developing the instinct necessary to do the job? If he is not, what do you do? More training, more time? Perhaps there is another assignment for which he is better suited and has more of an instinctive understanding of what is necessary for success. All people shine under different circumstances. Your instinct should be able to guide you through these decisions so you can optimize your employees' performance and improve your bottom line. Your instinct will be most effective if you...

CHAPTER 20

Lesson: <u>Know Your Domain</u>
Or, "I stole that concept from the FBI."

The FBI adopted a strategy dubbed "know your domain." The strategy was initially applied to the FBI counterintelligence activities. It made perfect sense. Each FBI field office needed to know what important assets were located within its territory that espionage activities may be targeting. For example, what companies were producing technology that had dual-use purposes? That referred to technology that had a legitimate use in business but could also be used for weaponry, encrypted communications, or anything that posed a threat to our national security. If we did not know what was in our own backyard, then how could we protect it? After we identified those assets, we were to determine who may have been seeking to obtain that technology or classified information, and then determine if we had those people roaming around our area. For national security purposes, I will not expound on this topic anymore, but I think you get the idea and can see how that concept can apply to all the violations the FBI investigated.

In the police department, you had to know your domain very well. In police jargon, the domain was your "beat." You had to know what stores and businesses were there, their addresses, and how to get there quickly. You had to know their vulnerabilities. For example, our friend the Coffee Stop stores, open all night, were targets of robberies, depending of course on whether there were cops inside drinking coffee. Certain restaurants that stored expensive foods or wines were subject to burglaries in the middle of the night. If there was a domestic dispute occurring at the same home night after night, it was important to recognize the address when given over the radio. You needed to know who the parties were, their propensity for danger, and what special precautions to take. You had to know the regular troublemakers by sight. Often, when you would see one of them, he was not really doing anything that would give you the right to stop him. If you knew his name, you could call it in on the radio to see if there was an outstanding warrant for him. If so, you knew what you had to do. If not, you saved yourself some unnecessary trouble. You just had to know when something was unusual or suspicious.

When I was on the police SWAT/anti-crime team, many times at night we had to follow burglary, robbery, or rape suspects. Late at night, it was hard to follow someone without being noticed, as there wasn't much traffic on the streets. Although our target could not see anything but headlights in the rearview mirror, if he saw headlights follow him down each street and around each turn, the surveillance was blown. Obviously, we didn't know the intended path of each person we followed. We had to maintain surveillance without being spotted, or our efforts were worthless. To do that, we often had to "back off"—turn off the street and let someone else pick it up down the road. If we did not know where the next turn was or if the road split up ahead, we were asking for problems. Our success depended upon knowing our domain.

Somewhat related to risk management, to know your domain is to know your threats and vulnerabilities. To do an assessment of your internal threats, bring out your SWOT team—not the SWAT team, that may frighten some employees. SWOT stands for Strengths, Weaknesses, Opportunities, and Threats. Analyzing the following categories will help you develop a blueprint for recognizing weaknesses and threats and capitalizing on your strengths and opportunities. This is one of many variations of SWOT analysis techniques:

Strengths

- Efficient processes
- Proprietary information
- Public perception of your strengths
- Marketing expertise
- New products or services
- Location
- Reputation

Weaknesses

- Reliance on a few key customers and/or vendors
- Lack of new products or services

- Location
- Inferior distribution channels
- Inefficient processes
- Damaged reputation

Opportunities

- Emerging markets
- Strategic partnerships
- Innovative research and development
- Business failure of a competitor

Threats

- Competition
- Competitive intelligence gathering
- Changing technology
- High debt
- Poor cash flow
- New regulations

By listing each component with specificity, plan a course of action in response. For example, if one of your weaknesses is your limited number of vendors, then you put together a network of vendors who can meet your needs. Then, you are not susceptible to price manipulation by one vendor or business interruption should that vendor's business fail. This sounds basic and obvious, yet so many companies do not recognize these threats, or take protective action until after the problem surfaces.

Watch those PESTs. PEST is an acronym that stands for Political, Economical, Social, and Technological; these are potential external threats outside of an organization's control, of which it must stay aware and react to change. Follows are a few examples of these PESTs:

<u>Political</u>

- Changing compliance requirements
- Trade agreements
- Political instability
- Governmental policy shifts
- Activism
- War

<u>Economic</u>

- Financial stability
- Market risk
- Credit risk
- Interest rates
- Taxes
- Economic policies

<u>Social</u>

- Demographic shifts
- Lifestyle changes
- Changing ethics and mores
- Religious and cultural issues

Technological

- Obsolescence
- Access to information
- Privacy and security
- Intellectual property rights

As with SWOT, identify your PESTs, know the potential risks and take proactive action.

Do you know your domain? Do you know what the threats and vulnerabilities to your company are? Internally, do you know when your office is not functioning as effectively and efficiently as usual? Do you know when certain employees are not as productive as usual? There are little things that may not be apparent but affect productivity. For example, is someone who usually brings up the esprit de corps not doing so lately, and morale is affected? Has there been a new employee introduced to the team who has had a negative effect on morale?

You most likely notice trends from comparative reports, such as revenue or production numbers. Externally, are you watching movements in the marketplace or local and world affairs that may affect your business? Know what to expect, and when a normal pattern changes, inquire. Then take action!

Did the colonists beat the superior British forces because most of the integral fighting occurred in their own backyard? They knew the terrain, and they knew each other.

They knew their domain. Did 9/11 occur because we did not know our domain—did we fail to identify threats surfacing in our backyard? What businesses have failed because they did not see emerging trends and changing tastes, styles and technology occurring in their own backyard? Have companies failed or at least suffered from internal thefts, leaking of trade secrets, investments in products that failed to sell, or not seeing the competition creeping up on them, especially in the world of high tech? The International Chamber of Commerce estimates losses attributable to intellectual property theft in excess of $600 billion per year. Can we afford that? Failure to stay alert will cost you.

Know your people. Know your company's "personality" and watch for changes. Stay alert. Listen. Know your domain.

CHAPTER 21

Lesson: <u>Do You Fix Your Broken Windows?</u> Or, "Do you believe in the Broken Windows Theory?"

Many of us have heard about the Broken Windows Theory credited to criminologists James Q. Wilson and George Kelling. In simple terms, the theory addresses the causes of crime using a building with broken windows as an example. If a building is left with a few broken windows that do not get repaired, people will tend to think that nobody cares about the buildings or the windows, and that breaking a window is OK. Then someone who is predisposed to such an act will break another window. Then another window is broken. Before you know it, the building is broken into, vandalized and perhaps set on fire, because of the message that such crimes are ignored. This message then spreads, and crime proliferates. The Broken Windows Theory reached its height of popularity in the mid 1980s. It started with the New York City Transit Authority pursuing what traditionally had been considered small crimes such as graffiti and fare jumping. The philosophy then spread to the New York City Police Department, where small, "quality of life" crimes were prosecuted. What followed was an overall drop in crime.

I was first exposed to the theory of broken windows before I ever heard of it, without realizing it and before it became so well known. The year was 1980, and I was a rookie police officer in Fairfax County. I was with my training officer, and we were working the night of Halloween. Then we got the call—a robbery had occurred. We responded to the home of the complainant. A young girl, perhaps ten years old, had her bag of Halloween candy taken from her by a little boy of maybe eleven years old who lived down the block. There was no hitting or violence involved, but he did grab it from her forcefully, against her will. That constituted robbery. My thought, which I properly kept to myself, was why didn't the father just go down there and talk to the boy's father? I also thought of being that age back in New York City during Halloween. If that was all that had happened to me, then I would have considered it a good night. I knew what the boy did was wrong, but for someone who grew up in New York, this was not big deal.

My training partner had a much different reaction than I had. He was upset over what had occurred. He drove over to the boy's house and confronted the boy and his parents. Naturally, the boy denied taking the candy. At that point, I was ready to leave and move on to some "real police work." My partner stayed at it and pressed the boy. He did it professionally and in a low-key way so the parents would not become too defensive and ask us to leave. Eventually, the boy confessed. My partner laid into the parents. He explained how the boy could be charged with robbery in juvenile court. He took the parents aside and explained how this could progress to worse crimes. The parents seemed genuinely concerned, and a bit afraid. We left with the parents agreeing to counsel their son and then apologize to the little girl and her family. We went back to the little girl's house, and everyone seemed satisfied. I thought my partner did a good job, but I still had a hard time justifying all that police time spent on what I thought was such a small issue. I told my partner how minor this seemed to me, compared to my life in New York City. "That's just the point," he said. "We don't want to become New York City." It was a good point, but I shrugged it off.

The next weekend, I drove up to visit my parents in Queens, NY. Saturday night, I went out with an old high school girlfriend. We were walking around Times Square in Manhattan when we passed a corner where a group of fifteen to twenty young men were gathered, acting aggressively and obnoxiously playing their "boom boxes." For those too young to know that term, that was simply a big radio that was able to blast loud music. This was long before the iPod.

The miscreants were loud and spewing out crude remarks to my female companion. Naturally, I wanted to confront them, a natural reaction for any man, especially one who was a cop. I may have even been armed; or maybe not, because it was illegal in New York City for even an out-of-state cop to carry a weapon. Being significantly outnumbered, and not willing to get pummeled over some crude remarks, realistically, what was I going to do? Finding it quite intimidating, I realized that I had no choice but to endure it.

Then I saw two cops sitting in their car. They could see what was happening. I wondered why they were not out on the street confronting this crowd. Then I realized this was New York City; cops were not going to bother with just some loud, obnoxious group on a street corner. All of a sudden, I understood what my training partner tried to explain to me. Maybe if New York City addressed the little things in life, as we did in Fairfax County, New York City would have the nice standard of life we had become accustomed to and expected in Fairfax County. I did not realize it, but my partner had artfully employed the Broken Windows Theory. Years later, then Mayor Giuliani was credited with implementing the Broken Windows Theory and significantly reducing the crime rate in New York City.

Two great books discuss the Broken Windows Theory. Author Malcolm Gladwell in the *Tipping Point* and authors Steven D. Levitt and Stephen J. Dubner in *Freakonomics* present very different points of view on the subject.

How does the Broken Windows Theory affect you in business? Do you have little problems that arise during the day? These would be such things as minor violations of the rules, letting something "slip between the cracks," or personal conduct that is offending other employees. As with our children, we pick and choose what conduct we want to discipline; we have to pick and choose our fights. To go after every small deviation from our expectations would be too time-consuming and exhausting. Are you ignoring "quality of work life" issues that you should be addressing for the benefit of the majority of your employees? As we discussed, many managers shun personal confrontations.

What do you do about someone who comes in just a few minutes late every morning or from lunch? It is only a few minutes, but those minutes add up, and you are paying for nonproductive time. You justify it to yourself by saying, "It's only a few minutes; what's the big deal?" Or, you say to yourself that you don't want to appear petty. What tone is that setting? How is that affecting your control environment? Will others follow suit and start fudging a few minutes here and there? Then there is the snowball effect. If a few minutes late is OK, how about taking home a few company-owned items such as staplers, hole punchers, etc? Alone, each is worth minimal value. Just like the few late minutes, what's the harm? Pilferage spread out in small amounts throughout the company, over the years can really start affecting the bottom line. By the time you feel the pain, the problem is widespread.

There is the well-known business story of how a Delta Airlines employee noticed that the one piece of lettuce on the meals that Delta served was rather unappealing. By removing that one piece of lettuce from each meal, the airline ultimately saved over one million dollars annually. That was a cost reduction, benefiting the bottom line. Let's imagine that someone was stealing that one piece of lettuce, and it had to be replaced. If one missing piece of lettuce went unaddressed, then so would two and so on. Eventually, that one piece of lettuce could evolve into costly shrinkage. You do not want to send the message that it is acceptable to take that one piece of lettuce.

The term *exponential* has become quite hackneyed when trying to explain rapid growth. However, exponential growth is important when explaining the problem of not addressing small issues before they become big ones. While your business problems may or may not be empirical and able to be graphed, the following is just an illustration to drive the point home. Things may change slowly, almost imperceptibly, and then there will reach a point where its change is neither gradual nor linear, but truly exponential— growing by multiples of itself.

There is a fable of a king who was looking for a suitor for his daughter. He offered all the young men who came to compete for her hand the same offer. Work for me for 30 days. I will pay you $10,000 a day or I will start with a penny on the first day and double it every day. Each man accepted the former and was readily dismissed by the king. As the king worried that there were no men wise enough for his daughter, another potential suitor came forward. The wise young man who chose the latter offer, received the king's daughter's hand in marriage. Why?

Determining pay at $10,000 a day for 30 days is simple math, $10,000 X 30 = $300,000. Not bad for a month's work. To start at a penny a day, then double that penny each day for ten days would yield a daily pay of $5.12 with a total of $10.23 earned to date, compared to $100,000 on the other plan. So far, the double penny plan sounds like the wrong choice. On day twenty, under the double penny plan, one would get paid $5,242.88 for a total of $10,485.75 compared to $200,000; again, the double penny plan sounds like the wrong choice. By day 24, with the 30 days shortly ending, the double penny plan would pay $83,886.08 for a total pay of $167,772.15 versus $240,000. So late into the month, the double penny plan has still left you behind the $10,000 per day option. Clearly, this supposedly wise man made a poor financial decision. However, on day 25, things change. The double penny plan pays $167,772.16 for a total yield of $335,544.31. The $10,000 per day plan has yielded $250,000 at that point. By day 30, the total pay of the double penny plan would equal $10,737,417.60 compared to $300,000. Which was the better plan? The double penny plan did not prove beneficial until more than 80% of the month had passed. Then, in the little remaining time, the difference became substantial. Appearing incremental, something small became something big exponentially. Rapid changes can occur for good things or for bad things; unfortunately, as life goes, it is usually the bad things that seem to keep growing. Pay attention to the small things before they grow exponentially.

How small things can lead to big things was highlighted during my police years and can be illustrated by what happened one night while I was working anti-crime with the

SWAT team. We were conducting a surveillance in search of someone who was breaking into and burglarizing homes at night. I was stationed on the top floor of a building that overlooked the neighborhood that had experienced numerous burglaries. After several hours of a boring, uneventful surveillance, I noticed a white male running through a wooded area adjacent to an apartment complex parking lot. I did not know exactly what he was doing, but I thought it prudent to radio that information to our units on the street, requesting that one of our unmarked cars head to the street at the opposite end and try to catch up to this guy.

One of our team was quick to respond and stopped him. A moment later, I saw a security guard running in that direction, and I called that in on the radio as well. Another one of our team found the security guard and took him over to where we were holding the white male. We learned that the security guard had noticed the man trying to break into an apartment and was in pursuit.

We made a good arrest that night. My lieutenant, my sergeant, and all the cops on the team showered me with compliments for a job well done. Truly, I did not understand the kudos. All I did was to observe something and call it in on the radio. Someone else apprehended the burglar. After confiding to my close friend on the team that I didn't feel deserving of all the praise, he explained it to me.

"You had the shittiest assignment tonight, sitting up in that room, staring through those friggin' binoculars all night. You didn't complain, and you didn't even ask to switch off. You just did it. Most of us would have lost attention or maybe even fallen asleep. You stayed alert and responded quickly. Because of you, we got a serial burglar off the streets tonight. You did a great job."

OK, I accepted that compliment and enjoyed the praise of my more senior fellow police officers for whom I had great respect, still believing that the praise was not deserved. Only years later did I understand what they were getting at. Working narcotics on a team that relied heavily on each other and then especially later on in management, I saw how each person could contribute to the team's success or failure, with little effort. One individual can make a significant contribution to society just by doing his job properly, as we have seen from the heroics of airline pilots and ship captains. If every worker and manager in the workforce recognized that, the productivity and effectiveness of any organization could increase by a large margin, maybe exponentially.

Do not let small problems turn into big ones by ignoring them out of fear of confrontation. These problems may grow exponentially, literally or at least figuratively, and then spin out of control. Think about the impact of the issue on a macro scale—long-term effects, employee morale, sending the wrong messages, your control environment and ultimately, your bottom line. Fix your broken windows. Everything you learned will have to coalesce when you plant your...

CHAPTER 22

Lesson: <u>Boots on the Ground</u>
Or, "Now I've got to put it all together."

When a crisis strikes, or at the moment of any critical event, all that we have discussed must be brought together seamlessly and as effortlessly as possible. At the helm, coordinating the multitude of responsibilities and activities must be the CEO or the highest-ranking executive available to respond. Exxon CEO Lawrence Rawl received negative media coverage for not immediately responding to the scene of the Exxon Valdez oil spill in 1989. In 2005, the media criticized President George W. Bush for not returning immediately from vacation when advised of the destruction caused by Hurricane Katrina. The president and Rawl may have had very good reasons for their responses, but the public perception was one of disengagement. The boss must plant his boots firmly on the terra firma and assume responsibility for managing the crisis.

A major crisis occurred about two months after I reported as SAC. While at a training seminar in Maryland about thirty miles outside of our nation's capital, I was just sitting down to have dinner when my assistant special agent in charge called. "Boss, we've just had a bad shooting," he told me. I didn't know what that meant. Were agents killed?

Did our agents kill somebody? Within one second, a number of horrifying scenarios went through my mind. He went on to tell me that there had been a shooting at a high school up on the Red Lake Indian Reservation. We did not have all the information, but we knew that a number of students had been killed.

Rushing back to my room to try to book myself on the next flight out proved fruitless. The last flight for that day was leaving in less than half an hour. I could not have possibly made it. For a moment, I wondered if, at that point, my returning was even necessary. By the time I got there, the investigation would be well under way. Then I quickly realized that not responding was not an option; I was the boss and there was a crisis; I needed to be there. At 3:00 a.m. the next morning, I found myself with eyes wide open, anxious, unable to fall asleep and waiting for the 3:30 alarm to ring.

During my trip back to the office and then continuing to the reservation, I planned out everything I needed to do upon my arrival, step by step. When actually arriving on the scene, I quickly learned that all those plans had to change.

The first thing I noticed upon arriving at the scene on the reservation was the swarms of media waiting for a press conference. My media representative immediately approached me and warned me that I had better get briefed quickly and hold a press conference. The media, he cautioned, was like a hungry beast; they must be fed or they get hungry, go searching for food and become trouble. Before

I could speak to the media, I had to get all the facts I could absorb and prepare for some tough questions.

Upon meeting with my senior staff, I learned that we had just experienced the worst school shooting since Columbine, with five students, a teacher and a security guard killed, the gunman dead from a self-inflicted gunshot wound and there were a number of casualties. All of the survivors were out of the school building. The FBI SWAT team cleared the building to assure there were no "booby traps" or anyone else hiding in there. After the SWAT team finished, the building was secured so that the Evidence Response Team could begin a very detailed forensic examination, retracing the gunman's steps, determining bullet trajectory, collecting evidence including blood samples, and reviewing the school's videotape. Despite the sophistication of the forensic technology, the primary method of determining the facts would be interviewing witnesses and people who knew the gunman. Although the gunman was dead, we still had to treat this as any other crime scene, as if there was going to be a prosecution. We also learned that the gunman's grandfather and the grandfather's live-in companion were found dead in the grandfather's house, from gunshot wounds.

While preparing to hold the press conference, I was approached by one of my staff, known as a victim-witness specialist. Although that is a rather self-explanatory title, this job was to assist victims and witnesses through the criminal justice system and processes. The specialist would assure that they were informed of trial dates and other developments that could be released. If necessary, the specialist would arrange transportation to court or for counseling. When the program was introduced into the FBI, it was met with derision, considered a too liberal, social-service-oriented function for a law enforcement agency such as the FBI. Over the years, I hope we have been enlightened enough to see the benefits of such a program.

My victim witness specialist asked me not to do the press conference first. Given the warning of my media rep, I could not imagine why not. She explained that many family members of the victims were being sheltered and provided for in a separate building. I should go there, introduce myself, assure them of our commitment to this matter, and most importantly, tell them what I was planning to say in the press conference. She also told me that the families should not be surprised by anything I was going to say to the media and to allow them to express their opinions regarding the press conference. I understood and agreed with that, but there were other consideration. First, I knew that there were strained relationships between the FBI and the Native American community. I was not confident that my presence would be welcome or appreciated at this moment. Second, while I was sensitive to the families' feelings and wanted to avoid causing any more grief, I also did not want to get into a negotiation about the press conference. The intensity of their emotions would, understandably put their opinions at odds with what I felt was necessary to say. While I was never a big proponent of the generic term, *the public's right to know,* this was certainly a time when I felt we had an absolute obligation to tell the public as much as we could, while maintaining the privacy of the victims and families and assuring the integrity of the investigation.

When I went into the room to meet the families, I was not prepared for what I saw. No one was crying, but the grief that was on the face of each and every family member was overwhelming and told a very sad story. For a moment, I was overtaken by emotion and was speechless. After introducing myself, I told them what the investigation would encompass and what I was planning to say at the press conference. I welcomed their feedback and input. I received none; just the blank stares of distress. Probably, they were too much in shock to even speak or think about such things. Only months after this incident did I hear about how much the families appreciated given the opportunity to express their feelings, though they were too distressed to offer anything. I was glad I listened to the advice of my victim-witness specialist.

After that brief meeting, I immediately went off to the press conference, to give it all the energy and attention it deserved. Given my years in management, I had appeared before the media numerous times. Generally, I enjoyed press conference and even looked forward to some of the professional sparring that went on. All in all, I found the media easy to work with, professional and polite as they tried to do their job, which was to get information. You just had to know how to play the game with them. This was clearly going to be different than any other press conference I had ever had. Emotions were running high, even for the media. Other than the facts of the shooting, I was not quite sure what they were expecting to hear from me. Despite my personal feelings, representing the FBI, I could not appear overwhelmed with emotion; that would be unprofessional. Aware of my personality traits—I was not known for being warm and fuzzy—I was also concerned that I would appear too dispassionate. That would come off as insensitive, uncaring and detached. I did not want to give any reason to believe that I, or anyone in the FBI was that cold and indifferent to so much suffering. As is usual in life, I had to find the right spot somewhere in the middle.

I began the press conference by expressing sympathy to the families and the communities on behalf of the entire law enforcement community. I knew that we did not know everything about what had happened; there was still a lot of information that we had to determine. We knew that nine people had been killed, who they were, and that the gunman had committed suicide. I invited senior law enforcement officers to stand with me at the press conference to establish their presence and importance.

I told the media that we believed the gunman acted alone but that we would assure that a Columbine-like conspiracy was not about to unfold. While I did not want to start a panic at the suggestion that there may be threat of continued violence, I also did not want to minimize the importance and implications of a second murder scene.

The grandfather was a police officer of the tribal police. Now there was an even greater impact on the community.

After I briefed the media on all the facts, they began asking many questions. I did not realize that the press conference was being aired live around the world. The questions the media were asking were surprisingly specific as to the gunman's lifestyle, use of the Internet, and other personal issues. Obviously, the media had done their homework. They knew things we did not know. On the surface, that sounds terrible for the FBI, but there are reasons for this. The media takes the swarm approach. They rush out and start asking questions to anyone who might know anything worth reporting. Trying to get their coverage out there first, they do not have to vet the information for accuracy or reliability as does the FBI; they do not have to document each conversation for later use; they do not have to worry about the integrity of evidence; they do not have to put a prosecutable case together; and they will not be held accountable for their actions as will the FBI.

When addressing the media, I always took the approach: tell them what we know, tell them what we do not know, and then tell them what we are planning to do and accomplish. I never bluffed; the media was quite savvy and would see right through it. When they did, they would beat you up and take your lunch money. This was definitely one time when honesty was the best policy.

During the press conference, I was asked several questions to which I did not know the answer. The media will always keep pushing for an answer, but you cannot allow them to corner you like that, or you will wind up eating your words. Actually, the questions the media were asking at Red Lake were really serving as a valuable source of intelligence. As I was answering, or not answering, their questions, I was forming an investigative strategy in my mind. The questions they were asking were clearly the result of information that they had dug up before we had. We used their strengths to our advantage.

At the end of the press conference, I named and thanked each agency that had responded to the scene to offer assistance. Such a small gesture gave each agency equity in the investigation and helped build the team concept. It also dispelled the myth of the FBI seeking all the credit at everyone else's expense.

After the press conference, it was time to focus on the intricacies of the investigation. We were definitely in the think-on-your-feet mode, and doing well. That is the strength of law enforcement officers; they are trained and experienced in taking the initiative, responding with alacrity, and acting intuitively. However, we quickly identified weaknesses in our processes that we needed to address. For example, all the law enforcement agents, FBI and otherwise, were running out on investigative leads as they came in, with no formal and centralized mechanism for recording who was where, who was covering what lead, and when it was completed. That was inefficient.

My senior staff was very supportive and patient and sat through a brain storming session, coming up with some quick fixes. We got hold of something as simple as a whiteboard and started listing all leads as they came in and to whom they were assigned. That gave us a little more control so we would know if something important was not getting done in a timely manner. Writing on a whiteboard was not ideal. We did not want all information posted where it was readily available to those who did not have a need to see it. As well, any accidental swipe of the eraser could have set us back significantly. We ordered our computer squad to head out immediately so we could get automated. All leads and intelligence were entered into a computer system that could control and store records of information and track progress.

The case agent was a senior agent who had worked on the reservation for a number of years. He knew the people and the culture. Meaning well, he tried to do it all. That was too much work for one individual. I did not want him bogged down with minutiae such as tracking leads, handling evidence, reviewing each report, etc. We needed him focused on the big picture. We assigned two agents as the intelligence team. Their job was to debrief each team as they returned from an interview, record all pertinent information and intelligence and weed out the minutiae. At around dinnertime, the intelligence officers, the case agent, my senior staff, and I met to discuss what we had learned and plan the next steps accordingly. There was only one way to disseminate all relevant information in an effective and efficient manner with so many people at the scene. Yes, the dreaded meeting.

These meetings were clearly necessary and purpose driven. Our first meeting was naturally the longest and probably most important. We assessed what we knew and what we needed to know. We also discussed logistics and determined what resources we had, what resources we needed, and what the general game plan was. Setting priorities was critical. Once we were confident that there was not an ongoing conspiracy and that more violence was not imminent, the top of our list of priorities was getting answers to the questions the media had posed to me. There was a reason they asked such specific questions. They knew something, and we needed to know what that was.

There was no time limit on the meetings, as all the information had to be shared and given adequate consideration for proper decision-making. We kept distractions to an absolute minimum. If we could put something on the back burner, we did so we could stay focused on the key issues. There was a lot of work to be done, so the meetings had to be efficient. There was no time for friendly banter or superfluous details; we had to stay on point. We did not meet as a group often, but when we did, the meetings were direct, to the point, and purpose driven. My senior staff, case agent and I met at least once a day. These meetings arose through necessity, not by scheduling. We were primarily interviewing juveniles, which created special legal concerns. Accordingly, we immediately engaged our chief division counsel for advice and guidance.

We set up a "war room" in a small office in the jail building, where prisoners and visitors were walking back and forth. That was challenging as privacy was of paramount concern. We had to be able to meet and speak openly while at the same time, we had to be cautious as leaks to the media or the public could derail our investigation. Cell phone coverage was spotty, so meeting in person took on greater importance to assure clear communication. The importance and sensitivity of every step we took required face-to-face communication; there was no room for misunderstandings. We wanted to assure that all parties who needed the information were getting it at the same time. If not, that could affect morale; we needed to assure a tight, cohesive team where nobody thought they were being cut out of the information flow, especially members of the other law enforcement agencies. Even though there were times when I wanted to meet with just FBI agents, I did not do that. The appearance of that would be misunderstood and destroy the feeling of team we had successfully created.

We also tried to use the meetings to convey that we understood the sacrifices that were being made and that we were all in this together. Good food was hard to find— bless the Red Cross, who tried to keep us well fed. We were far from home, and agents were staying in hotels. This was an intensely emotional investigation. There were personal issues affecting our staff that had to be recognized. Probably every agent wanted to get home that night just to hug their kids, but they could not. We had to be alert to the emotional impact on our own people. Listening to feedback was important; we listened for indicators of stress becoming a dominant factor either individually or on the team as a whole. We were alert for those whom we possibly needed to speak to in private. This related to the first of the internal controls. The meetings established the control environment. The tone of the investigation was one of compassion and understanding for the victims and the community; and one of mutual sacrifices, support and cohesiveness for ourselves. We would all share in the hardships and look out for each other. We were tired, dirty, hungry, and getting irritable. But we had to persevere without turning on each other.

The objectives were clear and definitive: learn all we could about the gunman and his actions that led to the carnage, determine if there was a conspiracy that would result in further harm or if anyone else was involved in planning this horrendous crime and collect evidence as if the gunman was still alive and this case was going to trial. That way, should any additional conspirators be identified, we would have a solid, tight case to present to the federal prosecutors. When all was said and done, the community was going to want to know exactly what happened. We had an obligation to provide those details to a point allowable by law.

How were those objectives communicated? Through the only way practical, those meetings. There were more than one hundred law enforcement officers from over twenty different agencies on the scene working. E-mails, phone calls, and word of mouth would not work. The only way to communicate to all of them simultaneously was a massive meeting. Obviously, we could not do that too often, so when we did meet, the agenda had to be defined, specific, complete, direct, and to the point, as everyone needed to get back to work.

Forming a partnership became critical. While the FBI maintained primary jurisdiction, we needed help. We had to consider the thoughts and feelings of the other agencies, which included local law and federal law enforcement agents. We were also joined by the Bureau of Indian Affairs (BIA), which worked under the Department of Interior. Most of the agents and I, had never worked with them before. I did not know what to expect. I met first with their boss, whom I will call Ed. I got lucky; Ed was a friendly, funny and generally nice guy. He had one goal, to do his job. He understood our respective roles and became a true partner within minutes. The BIA had one big advantage, all being Native Americans, they were better able to establish a rapport with the members of the reservation. They proved to be of great value in bridging the gap between the FBI and Native American community on the reservation. Knowing that, I would have been foolish to not include Ed in all the decisions and make him a full partner, as he best knew how the community would respond. Additionally, the BIA took over the police function of the tribal police to allow them time to grieve and deal with their loss. As the investigation continued, the partnerships became primarily one FBI agent and one BIA agent. We needed professional relationships and trust to build and thus watch a team develop.

While we were running and gunning in the think-on-your-feet mode, one of the first things we noticed was that we had to correct was the quality of some of the reports of interviews. They were quite rudimentary. As for information, we were getting a lot of information but not necessarily the right kind of information, the kind that would truly advance the investigation. The information and intelligence gleaned from the interviews was not being recorded in a systematic, methodical manner, consistent with FBI rules or in a manner that allowed it to be analyzed and disseminated to the rest of the team. This was not an efficient method for what we had to accomplish. The urgency of the situation had not changed, but we had to reassess our methodology.

The questions the interviewing agents asked covered how the people knew the gunman and if they heard him talk about shooting up the school, and left it at that. Many agents did not seem to grasp that we were trying to determine if a Columbine-like conspiracy was in the works. We also had to determine if there was anyone else involved, directly or indirectly. There may have been additional coconspirators who aided in killing the grandfather and his companion. Interviews were meant to be probing, to elicit new information, and to shed additional light on what we already knew. One of the problems we identified was that junior agents were partnered with other junior agents, sometimes from other agencies. We quickly corrected that. Senior agents were paired with the junior agents.

As the investigation unfolded, we learned that the gunman had engaged in hundreds of "conversations" over the Internet with many of his friends and classmates, discussing his desire and his plan to commit a school shooting. He displayed an obsession with the Columbine massacre. We found that he had set up a Web site where he created animations of violence that closely depicted what would become his demise. Unraveling was a story of a very disturbed young man. He possessed impressive artistic and poetic ability, but he was not concerned with his abilities; he just wanted to die, and take others with him.

We interviewed all the students who were familiar with the gunman or who had engaged in instant messaging computer conversations. We could not at that point, force anyone to talk to us. It would have to be voluntary, and we would need the parents' consent. Perception became important. If we were perceived as overly aggressive, trying to target and find guilt with these juveniles, we would not have elicited any cooperation. However, helping to overcome that was the lingering, subliminal message that they would not want to appear uncooperative to the community in such a sensitive, intense matter. We had to be perceived as interested only in getting the facts, which was the truth. Getting the parents to bring the juveniles did not prove extremely difficult. Getting the juveniles to open up to us proved more difficult. They were afraid; they were in shock; and they were experiencing grief. While it may seem that they should have been given time to deal with these emotions before being subjected to an FBI interview, that is not correct. We needed the information while it was fresh in their memories or before their recall of events changed, intentionally or unintentionally. Relying on memory, especially of traumatic events is risky in the investigation business. Getting at those memories early reduced that risk.

The difficulties of interviewing teenagers, and separating fact from perception proved challenging. It was time to seek advice and listen. I requested experts from our Behavioral Sciences Unit fly up immediately and help us prepare a plan for interviewing the juveniles. To protect FBI methods, I will not delve into the advice we were given or the plans we implemented, but their expertise clearly facilitated the process, and we began to get a lot of information from these juveniles. We learned that many of the students had heard of the gunman's plan to shoot up the school. Almost all of them said that they did not take him seriously, but we had some doubts about some of the students. We were convinced that the gunman acted alone but we were not sure that others did not help him plan and encourage him.

At one point, we received information that we thought would change the course of the investigation and send us off in a new direction. One young, teenage girl told us that she and the gunman were part of some cult that engaged in group sex and self-mutilation. This was unlike anything we had heard up to that point. Perhaps it would shed some light on these senseless murders, perhaps implicate others. It did seem out of character from all we had been told. However, the girl was adamant and on the surface sounded credible. We showed the report to one of our behavioral scientists. Fortunately, she was one of the FBI's best and was quite renowned for her work in profiling. She read the report and in about two minutes said, "I don't think so." She did not buy it. She told us that this just did not sound consistent with what we had been hearing and we needed to revisit this before spending any time pursuing this information. Was that training or was that just pure instinct?

That is why we called for the experts, to listen to them. We sent out our agents and re-interviewed the young girl, from a more skeptical perspective. She admitted it was all a lie. Why did she do this; what was her motivation to say disparaging things not only about the gunman, but about herself? It all started when the media came around looking for information, any information. This girl saw her chance for fifteen minutes of fame. This was the story she made up for the media, so she thought she'd better tell us the same thing. This goes back to why the media seemed to have more information than we did. They do not have to move with the same level of caution that law enforcement does. What was at risk of this false information? Mostly a lot of wasted time, and time was a precious commodity. Luckily, we managed to avoid that. We were concerned about other risks. That brings us to the next big concern we had—risk management.

After interviewing most of the juveniles, it became apparent that we needed to seize their computers. We were looking for evidence of exchanges of e-mails and instant messaging between the gunman and the students. This would possibly yield more evidence of a conspiracy, implicate others, and let us know if more violence had been planned for after the initial rampage. We wanted everyone to hand over his or her computers voluntarily. For many, we did not have probable cause and could not force them to cooperate. For a few, we did have probable cause to get a search warrant and seize the computer, against their will if necessary. We did not want to do that. Raising the hostility of the community was not in anyone's best interest; this would pose a serious risk to getting the cooperation we so desperately needed. Also, while we were starting to focus on certain juveniles over others, we did not want to tip our hand as to who we were looking at more closely. If the community started to suspect certain individuals were involved in these murders, we would have to be prepared for the possibility of retaliation and violence against those individuals and their families, another obvious risk. The BIA took the lead responsibility for assuring everyone's safety on the reservation. Assessing our risks, both internally and externally, was consistent with the second internal control, risk assessment.

We managed to convince everyone to bring in the computers voluntarily. One juvenile destroyed the hard disk before we could get to it. The plan was to collect the computers and fly them back to our office so our cyber experts could start reviewing them for evidence or lead information. Problems arose as we started collecting the computers. Agents took possession of the computers and left them sitting unattended somewhere to be picked up as evidence. Paperwork was incomplete or missing. Remember, we discussed the importance of what we call the "chain of custody" for evidence. Now we had risks within our internal controls concerning the third internal control, control activities. The information on the computers had the potential of being vitally important evidence. We could not risk tainting the integrity of the evidence.

Rather than chasing after each agent after he took custody of a computer and trying to correct the paperwork after the fact, we went proactive. We flew our evidence technician up to the reservation. We implemented a procedure requiring that when an agent took possession of a computer, he brought it directly to the evidence technician. She checked all the paperwork and assured the chain of custody was in order before releasing the agent. Then we flew the computer back to our office. That system worked. We identified an internal risk and mitigated it.

For my senior managers and me, there was no choice here but to multitask. There were just so many things to be cognizant of. We had to see the forest and the trees. Putting the case together and determining if there was an ongoing conspiracy was clearly the priority. But we had to watch all the other issues—legal issues especially with minors, health and well-being of our employees, handling of evidence, possibility of violence on the reservation, media—and there was still an FBI office to run with all the other responsibilities we had. White-collar crime, terrorism, and bank robberies did not take a break while we investigated this one tragedy. The only way to accomplish this was through the fourth internal control, information and communication. Staying close to my management staff during this time was more critical than ever. As they would receive information reported up the chain of command, they would take appropriate action and inform me if necessary, weeding out the superfluous and insignificant data. We spoke often and discussed issues as they arose. We even argued—professionally of course; I always encouraged dissension. My subordinates knew they could disagree with me, and when they did, they always did so politely and respectfully.

As the investigation continued, we were surprised at just how many students had heard of the gunman's plan to commit the school shooting. At first, we thought it was only a few of his close friends, but there were many more than that. More than thirty students had at least heard of the plan. Most maintained that they did not take him seriously, yet others believed it would happen at a later date, perhaps on April 20 to coincide with the Columbine massacre, which, as we discussed, had become an obsession of the gunman. Simply knowing about the plan was not a crime. To charge a student as a conspirator, the prosecution wanted to be able to show at least one overt act. We could not find that, except regarding one student.

As the investigation progressed, we focused on one particular juvenile. We developed probable cause that he committed at least one overt act in furtherance of the shooting. We now had the ability to arrest him. Because he was a juvenile, we could not share any information with the media, and I still cannot share any information more than what has been said. At the time, the arrest was somewhat cathartic. After long hours and hard work, we proved that what we were doing was productive; our plan worked. The arrest was covered by the media in other countries. We felt good about the arrest. We were not happy that a young student had participated in such a horrifying act, but we were glad that we succeeded in getting to the bottom of what happened. That was then.

Now, years later, I look back at that decision with a more critical eye and believe that I should not have authorized my agents to make the arrest at that moment. Let us not have a misunderstanding. The arrest was legal, moral, valid, and necessary; it just should not have been executed at that very moment. In retrospect, I now believe that this was a knee-jerk reaction; we were anxious to show results. Why do I feel that way?

After the arrest, the community's perception of us seemed to change. Although anyone should realize that the FBI conducts an investigation with the possibility of arresting someone, everyone was sure that there was nobody else involved, certainly not "my child." Now, we were no longer viewed as just wanting to learn the facts, but wanting to arrest "your kid." While there is no way of knowing whether someone was deterred from offering information because of the arrest, there is also no way of knowing if someone would have come forward with more details. Many other juveniles knew of the gunman's plans, though most stated that they did not take him seriously. How truthful that was, we did not know. There was no reason to believe that any other juvenile was active in planning this carnage, or there would have been additional arrests, yet many of the agents believed that there were kids who knew more than what had been shared. At ages fifteen and sixteen, other children who directly or indirectly encouraged this horrendous tragedy, I feel, should have somehow been held accountable. That will not happen. While I do not think the timing of the arrest changed the ultimate outcome in any way, it should have waited.

The public and especially those on the reservation wanted to know all the facts. They wanted to know about the arrest. They wanted to know who else knew about the plan. Wanting to know was certainly understandable. We could not tell them. The law was very clear in this regard. We met with families of the victims about a year after the tragedy. The wounds had not healed. They could not accept that we could not share information with them. Some of the family members, though only a few, felt that the FBI did not treat them with respect for their emotions. We tried hard to be understanding and sympathetic, but unfortunately while investigating a mass murder, some of our actions unintentionally appeared just the opposite. While that may just be the unfortunate nature of the business, I was sorry to hear that.

The wounds of the Red Lake High School massacre run deep. I can only hope that the Red Lake Nation can find some comfort in the heroic actions of their students, faculty, and police.

After the dust had settled, I received numerous calls thanking and congratulating me on my leadership during this tragic event. Those calls were humbling, and I greatly appreciated them. Police chiefs, sheriffs, colleagues, community members, the media, even a congressman found the time to make such a nice telephone call. Importantly, at least to me, was from whom I did I not hear—my boss, the FBI director. A simple phone call would have gone a long way. If I had been a member of his inner circle—that team within a team—I suspect that his response would have been much different. The FBI is not free of corporate politics. I did hear from some other people in the FBI, whose opinions also meant a lot to me. Several agents thanked me for pushing them towards finding the truth; they did not believe that there was any conspiracy, just a lone gunman. One supervisor who had been on the scene, said to me, "Boss, thanks, I learned a lot about leadership from you at Red Lake." That was gratifying; sometimes the praise of your subordinates is more important than that of your superiors. We eventually conducted an internal after-action review of our response. We had an open and honest discussion. Every entity that was present at the scene was at the after-action review: the first agents on the scene, the case agent, the Evidence Response Team, the SWAT team, the computer squad, victim-witness specialists, support personnel, and management. We identified several aspects of our response that needed improvement. We implemented changes to our crisis management plan and felt that although we did an excellent job at Red Lake, our response next time would be even better. Continuous improvement is the path to success. Kaizen.

From managing this crisis, I learned just how important it is to take care of your team. You must show appreciation for everyone's efforts, whether they are in your inner circle or not. Through it all, there is one thing you must not lose sight of, though it sounds incongruous to the subject of tragedy. You must never lose your sense of humor. That does not mean that you will not be saddened by tragic events or that you should be insensitive to the feelings of others.

It does not mean that you should tell inappropriate jokes at inappropriate times. It does mean trying to keep your wits about you and encouraging the same of your team. As moved and saddened as we were at Red Lake, we still had to find time to laugh, privately of course, and obviously not at the tragedy, but usually at our circumstances or just at ourselves. The pressure must find an outlet. Self-effacing humor is usually the best kind.

Since Red Lake, there have been numerous school and workplace violence incidents, with the Virginia Tech massacre in 2007. In one day, in 2008, there were three separate workplace-shooting incidents. The deadly trend continued into 2009 with the murder of a Yale graduate student. The poor economy and massive job losses have possibly contributed to incidents of workplace and domestic violence.

After retiring and performing consulting work, I volunteered time to a religious institution that also had a school, in designing a safety and crisis management plan, driven to action by the Virginia Tech incident. To be able to minimize such threats, we planned a system whereby video cameras were installed throughout the facility. The cameras fed into the main office, where all cameras could be monitored simultaneously. While a given alarm would signal a lockdown for the entire facility, those in the office would be able to contact each individual room or office and advise of the threat location and whether fleeing the facility was advisable. This plan was not perfect, as none can be, but it was a solid and viable plan that may one day save lives. As we have discussed, you should have a crisis plan in the event of workplace violence or some other threat. Keep in mind that in a crisis, a person can only process a certain amount of information effectively; make sure your plan is not overly complex—remember to KISS.

Find balance in your plan; my motto: "Vigilance, sans paranoia."

Now, let's take a look at what we've discussed and see if all this plays out in a fictional, though realistic, business scenario. Let's…

CHAPTER 23

Lesson: <u>Meet Joe Bridges</u>
Or, "This could be me."

I am the district manager of the GoFar Moving Company with the day-to-day managerial responsibilities of the office. My office is on the West Coast. There are ten district offices throughout the country. I have been with the company for five years having come from one of our competitors. I answer to the chief operating officer, who is headquartered in a state about five hundred miles away. The chief operating officer reports to the CEO. Reporting directly to me are five shift supervisors, each of whom has approximately ten drivers under his supervision. We refer to these teams as crews. The nature of the work requires the crews to shift their workweek, sometimes working on weekends, just driving towards their destination with no time spent in the office. Because of the shifts, different supervisors and crews report to the office on any given morning for assignments. Some assignments are local and the driver will be back the next day. Some are trips that will require several days on the road.

I meet with my shift supervisors every Monday morning to go over assignments, determine how many moving vans are being deployed, and map out each driver's destination, travel route, and estimated time of arrival and return. We also discuss any general or personnel issues. I find these meetings imperative, as I must know what resources are available to handle work as it comes in. I allow a little banter about our weekends before the meetings but not more than a few minutes. The meetings always start on time and usually end within an hour.

We are a national firm, but our exposure is primarily local, moving residents and businesses in a tri-state area. We have moderate competition from about three other companies that offer similar services at competitive prices. Our company relies heavily on word of mouth and advertising mostly through the signage on our trucks. Operating out of our facility, we have about thirty moving vans on the road conducting business on any given day.

Today, Monday morning, I show up at the office at 7:30 a.m. after being on vacation all last week. To catch up and get current, I know I must prioritize my work. I decide to first check my e-mail on the company's intranet, so I am looking only for business-related e-mail. Personal e-mail can wait for another time or, preferably, on my own time. I have to sort through numerous e-mails and respond to as many as I can before the day's work really begins. Just by reading the first few sentences of the e-mail, I decide whether it is critical to address now or it can wait until I catch up.

Then I check my voice messages. Once again, I know by who is calling and by first few words whether the message is important, if I need to hear the entire message or can safely fast-forward to the next one. Out of courtesy, I try to return all phone calls that day, but even those need to be prioritized, and I may not get to return every call. I will call the next day. Any longer, I would perceive as rude.

Then I approach my overflowing in-box. Once again, it is the same exercise of recognizing what I need to know first, or at all, what needs to be addressed, and what can wait. I read the executive summary. Scanning the document, I read the first few sentences to determine the nature of the paper. I may read the first sentence or two of the next few paragraphs if I need to get a better idea of the message. Is it a new policy of which I need to be aware and/or disseminate throughout the office? Is it old stuff we already know? Is it regarding a meeting scheduled a month away and I can ask my secretary to set a tickler a few days in advance? Is it simply something I can delegate down to a shift supervisor? If follow-up is needed, again, I have my secretary set a tickler to assure the delegated responsibility gets done, or at least is in the process of getting completed in a timely manner. I leave little to my memory. To start my day, short of an emergency, I first get my communication responsibilities out of the way.

One of my steadier and more important corporate clients, Fred Blake from the Anderson Company, left a telephone message for me. He said he was concerned, and from his tone, he was apparently upset about a recent delivery we made for him. He alluded to some damage. I ask my secretary if she knows about the issue Fred was calling about.

She does not. I call him back promptly at 8:00 a.m., hoping to catch him before he gets too busy at work. He is not in, so I leave him a message.

Not too long into my morning, I will usually be approached by one of my subordinates with a problem. Usually, I can refer him back to his shift supervisor for a fair resolution. I have an open-door policy but prefer that all issues be resolved with their immediate supervisors if possible. Today, John Moore has a concern. As he comes in to see me, I tell him that I am waiting on a return call that I must take, and if it comes, I will need to interrupt our conversation. I want him to know that in advance, so if the phone call does come, John does not feel that I have been rude or dismissive of his problem. He understands. John is scheduled to work this coming weekend and would like to switch with someone as his young daughter has a dance recital out of town. Nobody is willing to switch with him because it is Super Bowl Sunday. He has spoken to his shift supervisor, who said that there was really nothing he could do about it. The supervisor is responsible for assuring the assignments are distributed fairly so that each driver does not have to be away more than others or, conversely, is away often enough to earn some reasonable overtime pay. John acknowledges that it is his turn to work on the weekend. Drivers are allowed to exchange assignments but are only forced to in true emergencies. This matter, while important to John, does not qualify as an emergency. I am a little flustered by John's request. John is not known as a true family man. He usually volunteers to take overnight trips to allow him a night out without his wife knowing what he is doing. I don't really like that kind of conduct, but he always does his job. I am not going to pass judgment on how he conducts his marriage as long as the company is not involved.

My visceral reaction is that John's request is disingenuous. I think he probably has his own Super Bowl party he wants to go to and is just making up the story of the dance recital. At first, my gut tells me to say that I cannot help him. There is just something indescribable about John today that strikes me, something inside me, some instinct that tells me to check into this a little more before saying no.

At that moment, my secretary interrupts to tell me that Fred from the Anderson Company is on the phone. John, remembering what I told him, politely gets up to leave. I ask my secretary to put Fred on hold for just one moment. I tell John that I will look into this and get back to him as soon as possible. He leaves with a smile and a "Thanks, Boss." After John leaves my office, I ask my secretary to have John's supervisor come see me at 1:00 p.m., then I get on the phone with Fred.

I already know that Fred is upset, so I think a little small talk might assuage his apparent concern with our service. I start out talking to Fred about the upcoming Super Bowl. Not being a sports fan I do not really have much to say, at least nothing intelligent. Since Fred is a sports fan, I let him talk me into taking the underdog on a $10 bet. I think that is a small price to pay for some goodwill.

Fred wants to talk about a problem his company had with a cross-town move last week while I was gone. He starts by saying, "I'm sure you know why I am calling." I am embarrassed to have to admit that I do not know why he is calling. Whatever the problem, it is big enough for him to wait for me to return to work and expect me to know about it first thing Monday morning. I do not like being caught off guard. Apparently, one of the drivers, Hal Fuller, had delivered a number of computers and equipment to one of Anderson's satellite offices. One of the monitors fell off a table because Hal placed it near the edge half on top of a book, causing the monitor to fall and crack the screen. Hal insisted that he placed it down properly and that the accident was the fault of one of Anderson's employees. Fred is mad that Hal denied responsibility, and Anderson wants us to reimburse them for the screen. I ask Fred if I can first speak to Hal before responding; it is only fair that I listen to both sides of the story. Fred agrees but asks for a call back within two days. I agree.

I call Hal's supervisor, who checks the board for Hal's whereabouts. Hal's supervisor knows immediately that Hal will be arriving at his destination at approximately 4:00 p.m. today. How does he know? We maintain a simple whiteboard tracking all such information. Of course, it is also entered into a computer, which can be accessed with a few keystrokes, but that interrupts any other work being done on the computer. It is much simpler and more efficient to just look at the board. High tech is not always the answer.

It is very important that every shift supervisor knows exactly what assignment each driver is on, his scheduled stops, and his expected arrival and return times. If a driver gets sick or if there is a vehicle breakdown or some other emergency, we want to know immediately where we need to respond and what authorities to call upon. We need to move quickly without having to gather a whole lot of facts.

I ask the supervisor to come see me in two hours to discuss the broken monitor matter. It is important because of who the client is, but it can wait a few hours while I address other work. While each driver has a cell phone, we try not to call and distract them except for emergencies. We won't be talking to Hal till at least 4:00 p.m. today anyway.

OK, so now I know I have two more issues that I have obligated myself to address today: see Hal Fuller's supervisor in two hours about the broken monitor and see John's supervisor about his weekend schedule at 1:00 p.m. Although my secretary has already noted these meetings, I mark them down on my desk calendar just so I do not inadvertently schedule something else at the same time. That's assuming, of course, that I look at my calendar.

I start on my in-box. The first piece of mail I encounter brings back memories. I, like the other district managers around the country, am being asked to review the annual renewal of the corporation's liability insurance coverage. We do this each year, and the district managers' task is to provide any ideas relating to coverage we should obtain or should drop. Identifying new vulnerabilities is an integral element of our risk management plan. We make suggestions only. The final decision is made at corporate headquarters.

I remember that right after September 11 we were encouraged by our insurance company to obtain additional coverage for acts of terrorism. We learned through the grapevine that all our competitors had signed on. Given the number of trucks in our fleet and the number of divisional offices, the premium was not immaterial. I recommended against it during a managerial video conference. I was accused of being naïve, almost of being unpatriotic, for not accepting that the terrorist threat was real. I understood what September 11 meant to our country, but I did not see this insurance as a reasonable expenditure for our company, and that was my focus—our company.

Less than a year later, I recommended that we do a risk/threat analysis, citing September 11 as a primary reason; we needed to determine if we were adequately protecting our personnel, material, and assets against the most likely threats. The risk/threat assessment was conducted by a professional, a retired FBI agent. The assessment made several important recommendations. The assessment noted that our company was not a likely target of terrorism. There were protective actions and policies we were able to implement to reduce the risks of fraud, theft, burglary, vandalism, and other such crimes. The likelihood of a September 11 attack against our company was not only low, but almost impossible for our company to protect against.

The next year, based on that assessment, we dropped the act of terrorism addition to our coverage. Rather than let rumors spread, we sent out a memo to all employees explaining our rationale. We expected a backlash, employees thinking we were not concerned with their safety. We received almost the opposite reaction. Employees seemed relieved that after carefully examining the situation, after stopping and thinking about it, we did not find that any of us were at unusual risk of being struck by terrorism. I had a great big "I told you so" just dying to come out. With my goal of one day becoming the chief operating officer, I wanted to impress the CEO. I resisted the urge. I think I would have sounded more foolish than impressive. The CEO probably remembered my recommendation and I believe it was reflected in my annual performance appraisal and year-end bonus.

Later that morning I get a call that reminds me to not so readily hand out my business cards at industry trade shows. A salesman wants to come by and show me the latest security devices for our fleet of trucks. He has very advanced and very expensive equipment, the latest high-tech gadgets. Fortunately, we have done our risk/threat assessment. Given the nature of our clients, our trucks rarely have unusual or highly valuable property to be moved. A truck hijacking, while possible, seems highly unlikely. The company has never experienced one in its twenty years of existence. Our drivers do not collect cash and do not have anything more than what is in their wallets. We do not seem to be at any particular risk other than the average risks of being out on the streets. We have already checked with our insurance carrier and these additional devices would not materially reduce our premiums. Drivers have been instructed not to resist any attempts at theft. We are not willing to put our employees at risk. When the drivers must park overnight, they use standard industry locking and alarm devices. We feel that we adequately assess our vulnerabilities and take appropriate precautions. I tell my secretary to tell the salesman that I am not interested, politely of course. I do not want him thinking that there is any reason to call me back.

Two hours pass quickly, and Bob Miller, Hal's supervisor, comes to see me as I had requested. I ask about Fred's complaint of the broken computer monitor.

"I knew he'd call, that whiner," Bob says.

Bob knows Fred and what an important customer he is. Obviously, Hal had reported the incident to Bob. Hal insisted that he had laid the monitor on the table safely and securely. One of Anderson's employees moved some desks to make room for the rest of the delivery and that's when the monitor fell. Hal was adamant that he was not responsible. According to Bob, Hal is a top-notch employee and an honest guy; there is no way Hal was lying.

I know Hal casually just through office conversation. I consider Bob to be a solid supervisor and I trust his assessment. I tell him to let Hal know that I will call him on his cell phone tonight to discuss the incident. I also tell Bob to let Hal know not to worry; we are behind him. I just want to hear about it directly from him. Bob is getting ready to leave, and I stop him.

"Bob, how come I didn't know about this before getting the call from Fred?"

"Well, Boss, you were out all week, and I just didn't figure it was worth bothering you."

"But you did suspect he would call, right?"

"Yes," Bob replied, "but it is Monday morning, and we haven't had a chance to speak yet."

"True, Bob, but you should have left that information with my secretary so I got it first thing this morning. I should not have been taken by surprise by such an important customer. That makes me look uninformed and disengaged from my business. Please don't let that happen again."

"Hey, I'm really sorry, Boss. You know I would never want to put you in a bad situation—" I stopped him.

"Bob, it's alright. I know you didn't mean any harm. Let's just learn from it and move on, OK?"

"OK, thanks."

Bob knows my style of communication. He walks away from my office confident that I said all that I needed to say and the issue is over. I do not expect it to happen again. I know I will have to talk to Hal and then call back Fred from the Anderson Company. Again, I tell my secretary to set a tickler for later in the day to remind me. As important as I consider this matter, I still run the risk of forgetting.

The morning flies by fast, and it is lunchtime. With no business luncheon plan, I just eat at my desk and get some paperwork done. It is 1:10 p.m. and John Moore's supervisor, Frank Wilner, is not in my office as scheduled. I ask my secretary to call him and have him report to my office. Just the call from my secretary sends the message: be on time!

I ask Frank about John's request to switch this weekend. First, I want to know if he really wants to attend his daughter's recital; it sounds out of character for him.

"I don't know," Frank continues. "We all want to be off for the Super Bowl, and nobody is willing to change, not even his good buddy, Gil Martinez, and they always help each other out. You know Moore; he's probably got some babe he wants to see while he tells his wife he's with the guys."

I think about this for a moment and am not quite sure what to make of it.

"What's Martinez's schedule today?" I ask.

"He's on a local run; he should be back around four today."

"OK, thanks. I'll talk to you later."

Having a driver work on a Sunday and miss the Super Bowl is a rather routine matter for our business; it just happens. John finding it important enough to go over his supervisor's head and see me is unusual, so maybe this is more important than I realize. Now I learn that his good friend is not willing to help him out. On the one hand, I'm suspecting that John is pulling a scam, and I don't like it. On the other hand, I don't want to jump to conclusions; something is just not right. Now there is something else I need to do at 4:00 this afternoon, only this has to appear unplanned.

The rest of the day proves to be rather routine and uneventful. I parcel out work requests, approve vouchers and expense accounts, review time sheets, take the normal phone calls that flow in, and read the voluminous corporate mail. Around 4:00 p.m., I take a casual walk to the locker room, where Gil, John's buddy, is packing up for the day. I stop by him to engage in social discourse and of course bring up the Super Bowl. I ask if he knows of anybody who might be willing to switch with John, though I try not to appear as if I know anything else.

"No sir, we've both asked around, and nobody wants to do it. I would do it for him, but I've already got a party planned, a lot of people coming over. I gotta be there."

"Yea, Gil, I would imagine. I'm sure John would like to be there too."

"Oh no. He wants to go to some performance his kid is doing. Look, he doesn't tell anybody this, but his marriage is on the rocks, and it's killing him. He's really trying to do these family things to patch things up. I hope he finds someone to cover for him."

"OK, thanks. Let's keep trying to get him a replacement."

"Sure thing, Boss. Thanks."

Well, it looks like my initial judgment was wrong. John's motivation is sincere. He is not playing me.

I call Frank, back into my office. I do not generally share personal information. I tell Frank that what I am about to tell him is confidential but important to carrying out our managerial duties, of which taking care of our people is a major role. I explain John's predicament and ask Frank to work hard to get someone to switch. I would like to offer an incentive but do not want to start a precedent for one employee. I tell Frank to get aggressive, to check with the other crews and try to find someone quickly. Certainly one driver will give up watching the Super Bowl for Sunday premium pay. I ask Frank if he was aware of John's personal situation. He was not. We try to stay out of our employees' personal lives, but a little informal conversation now and then can reveal a lot of important information to help us manage. In this case, if we can contribute to saving a marriage, we can possibly save an employee from going into despair and probably becoming a problem employee. An ounce of prevention... Not to mention that it just seems like the right thing to do. I suggest to Frank that if he had a little more interaction with his direct reports, he might have been aware of the situation and could have addressed it before it got to me. He acknowledges that. Like Bob earlier, he knows that this is all I have to say, and he gets the message.

It is now after 4:00, and I am getting ready to call Hal about the broken monitor. Grant Bailey, another shift supervisor, comes running into my office in a panic. One of his drivers, Ted Patterson, just had a rollover on the interstate.

It sounds bad; there are fatalities. He is about four hours away. I tell Grant that we need to get to the scene the fastest way possible, car or air, whatever works, and to bring at least two other shift supervisors and a number of our clerical personnel. I will notify corporate headquarters on the way; we need to move.

Grant quickly learns that getting a flight to the scene and transportation to and from the airport will take too long. We pack several people into three cars and head out. I call the chief operating officer while we are en route and tell him what I know, which isn't much. I suggest that he call the CEO and tell the CEO to head towards the scene given the possible magnitude of the accident. The CEO, Larry Franklin, conducts much of his business outside the office and is often traveling. He is well known in the industry, often speaks at industry conferences, and generally represents the company in a favorable light. His presence will be of great benefit during this crisis.

I had Carla Riggins, my most senior shift supervisor, stay behind and take over office operations in my absence. Not only is she the most senior supervisor and knows the business, but she has a good head on her shoulders; she is a good decision maker. She has an excellent reputation and is well respected by the other shift supervisors. Part of managing a crisis is assuring that the rest of the business continues on to the fullest extent possible, while addressing the crisis. Carla, who was at home at the time, is incredibly loyal to the company and responded immediately, no questions asked.

When we arrive at the scene, there is still mayhem. That part of the interstate is completely closed off as the police conduct their investigation. Of course, the other side of the interstate is backed up by rubberneckers. We know we can't drive right up to the scene, so we park the car off to the side of the road and walk over. This would not usually be considered a prudent move, but we have no choice; we have to get there. There is our moving van, rolled over, on top of another car. It is a tragic sight to see; it is emotionally painful as well. The police have a pretty tight border around the scene of the accident, and we have a hard time getting close enough to talk to any of the police officers in charge. I explain that we are with the moving company and can probably help answer a number of questions. They allow us in. The damage—broken glass, evidence of blood on the car—is overwhelming. It takes us all a few moments to regain our composure, which we barely do as we stand there in the light rain, the flashing red lights adding to the air of crisis.

On the drive up, I spoke to our legal counsel. Being realistic about liability, I was cautioned about what to say and not to say. At no point am I to acknowledge fault of the driver or the company. That is with good reason other than legal protection. I will not know all the facts for some time. I cannot truly assess fault, irrespective of how things look.

I learn that our driver, Patterson, had been arrested; he had alcohol on his breath. The driver of the other car had been killed. His wife and two children were taken to the hospital; their conditions are unknown. I leave one shift supervisor on the scene to assist in any way possible. Also, I want him to see if he can remove from our van any of Patterson's personal belongings or company property and paperwork before the van is towed. Obviously, that will be decided by the police.

I call Carla back at the office and have her send some of our staff to Patterson's house to offer comfort to his family and to drive them back here. She has already done that. I send another shift supervisor to police headquarters to be with Patterson. I head to the hospital with my clerical staff. By the time I get there, there are many family members, clearly in grief and shock. I go over and introduce myself. As expected, several respond with anger and will not speak with me. One or two others ask why I am there. I express my deep concern for what happened and tell them that I want to do all I can to help during this difficult time. After some tense moments, the family accepts my offer that my staff goes out to bring them back meals. We also arrange for hotel rooms for family members who come from out of town. All of that will be at the company's expense, naturally. I know I am going to exceed my spending authority, but I will have to face that later. I am confident that I am doing the right thing for the right reason.

The media has learned that I am at the hospital and is waiting outside. Naturally, they have questions about such a serious accident, especially with word going around that our driver has been arrested for driving while intoxicated. I call the chief operating officer and ask if the CEO is on his way. He says no; the CEO is on the East Coast and it is too late to get a flight out. I ask the chief operating officer if he, as second in command, is coming out to handle the media. "No, I'm not good with that media stuff. You'd better handle it. Just don't make us look any worse than we already do. We have a lot at stake here. Save our reputation."

I have never handled a press conference before. Being a district manager for a moving company doesn't usually offer many opportunities to be sought after by the press. I ask one of my shift supervisors to go out and tell the reporters that I will give a statement in about an hour. I think an hour will give me enough time to gather my thoughts and be able to answer some questions. The hour passes quickly.

I stand in front of a handful of reporters. I introduce myself and then say that our CEO, Larry Franklin, apologizes for not being here personally, but he is on the East Coast and cannot get a flight out. I explain all that we know at the time, which is that one of our vans had jackknifed and turned over on top of another car. I regrettably acknowledge the death.

"So what caused the accident?" is the first question asked.

I tell them honestly that I am not in a position to make that call; that will have to come from the police.

"We heard your driver was arrested for drunk driving. Can you comment please?" is the next pressing question, shouted out by a local news reporter.

I pause with that one. Then I realize I cannot honestly answer the question. I heard he had alcohol on his breath, but nobody ever said he was drunk. I acknowledge that he is in police custody, but as for any charges, they will have to ask the police. Then comes a question I am glad to answer.

"Has anyone from your company spoken to family members?"

Fortunately, I can honestly answer yes and go on to say what services we have offered them. That seems like a good way to end the press briefing. I say thank you and walk away, not taking any further questions.

Then I get a telephone call from Carla, back in the office.

"Joe, corporate headquarters suggested that they set up a war room with legal advisers, media consultants, and advertising execs, and that you call in every two hours to talk about what has transpired and what further response would be appropriate."

"Why would I need all that now? Look, nothing is going to happen every two hours to report. There is no need to have people standing by."

"Well, it gets worse, Joe. They also suggested sending out the chief operating officer to serve as liaison between headquarters and the events."

"I don't see it. There is no need for the chief operating officer to respond to the scene now. He was needed for the press conference, but that opportunity has already passed. Be nice, but definitely try to talk them out of it."

Fortunately, Carla does talk them out of it. I don't need a "war room." I certainly do not need the chief operating officer hanging around. His presence, at this point, will not offer any additional value. We have a process, and it is working. A new manager on the scene, who needs to be briefed and may have new and possibly uninformed ideas, will only add unnecessary complexity. We expect to be out of the area in a day or two; no need to complicate the situation. We have reached a point where things are as simple as possible, given the situation.

My staff and I will stay overnight and through the next day and I authorize the payment of fresh clothes and toiletries. We want to continue to support the family and also appear in court with our driver, Patterson. Corporate headquarters flies out an attorney to represent him. Patterson, when tested for alcohol consumption, was found to have been just under the legal limit. He was not charged with driving while intoxicated but given another much less serious citation. We post bond for him, and he returns home with his family the next day. As expected, that draws a loud cry from the family and some negative press coverage. When there is an innocent death, people want someone to blame and punish. Given what is known at the time, Patterson's release does not seem fair to the family. That is the law. We know that civil litigation is inevitable, and all further statements come from our legal counsel at corporate headquarters.

When I get back to the office, two days later, the first thing I do is hold an all-employee conference. I tell everyone basically what happened in terms of the accident. I acknowledge the death as a result of our van flipping over on to another car. I do not mention the alcohol; it is not my place to do so. I ask that nobody jump to conclusions and that they try to get things back to normal as soon and as much as possible. The story is a shock; we had never experienced anything like it. I publicly thank Carla for jumping in and taking over.

Then I decide to do a little background work on our driver Patterson. I find in his personnel folder that his supervisor, Grant, had twice noticed alcohol on Patterson's breath during working hours. I am glad that Grant had documented this fact, but he never brought it to my attention. I know that this is important information, and I forward it to corporate headquarters.

The next week passes by slowly. Finally, we get the news that the police investigation found that the accident was caused by another car cutting off Patterson. The highway was slick from the rain, and when Patterson tried to maneuver around the other car, he jackknifed and rolled over. Patterson was not held at fault. We all know that won't stop the civil suit that is to follow.

The CEO calls for a management retreat shortly after the accident. I think that is a great decision. It is important for all district managers to know what happened and to separate fact from fiction. I am to give a briefing of all that occurred, from beginning to end, and how it was handled. Basically, we are conducting an after-action review. The CEO runs it well; he places no blame and just wants to gather the facts and elicit opinions for forming a response plan should we have any such tragedies in the future. We realize that given the nature of our business, this should not have been an unexpected event. We should have already had a plan. We implement some new procedures. Shift supervisors must sit down with each of their drivers once a quarter and just see how things are going, sort of a progress review. Those reviews are then forwarded to the district manager. Headquarters appoints certain people to act as media representatives. We put together a crisis response plan that addresses a number of contingencies to include such accidents. That includes a response plan to support family members of our employees or members of the public who may have been harmed by our actions, directly or indirectly. District managers are given much higher levels of spending authority during such times, so as not to be concerned with that issue while trying to minimize damage. Corporate headquarters puts together a response team who would fly out immediately to offer logistical support so the district office would be able to maintain operations as normally as possible.

Following the retreat, I get periodic calls from corporate headquarters. First, they tell me that Patterson's future with the company is in question. Although not held at fault, and Patterson was not legally intoxicated at the time of the accident, he had been drinking. Our rules are very clear, documented, and had routinely been communicated to the employees: the consumption of any alcohol while driving a company vehicle is prohibited and is grounds for dismissal. Adding that Grant had observed this twice before, the company determines that Patterson is too much of a risk and potential liability to the company. He is fired.

I am then told by corporate headquarters that Patterson's supervisor, Grant, is also under scrutiny. He twice suspected alcohol consumption and did not take any further action than to document it. That is not sufficient and is deemed by the company to be highly negligent for a supervisor. Grant is also fired.

The next bit of bad news I hear directly from my boss, the chief operating officer, David Lyons. Corporate headquarters wants to know why I was not aware of the two memos Grant wrote about Patterson and are reviewing my culpability in this matter. I explain that I was never advised. Then I am asked if I ever look through the employee personnel folders. I say no, those are the responsibility of the shift supervisors. If there is something wrong, they should come to me; I am not required to review their folders. That is my defense. I can tell that the chief operating officer is not really satisfied with my responses. I spend many sleepless nights waiting to hear what corporate headquarters will decide about my fate. I finally get the call from my boss.

"Joe, headquarters spent considerable time trying to figure out what you did or did not do that contributed to the accident. The arguments you made about the shift supervisors being responsible for bringing information to you were only half right."

"Well, Dave, is that half good or half bad?" I ineptly and inappropriately try to interject some lightheartedness.

"Unfortunately, probably more half bad, Joe. While you weren't required to review the drivers' personnel folders, you should have. At least on occasion, without notice, you should've just looked through them, sort of a surprise audit."

"Surprise audit? On personnel folders? I never would've even thought about something like that. I can't imagine what would make me think about doing that."

"You were the district manager, and that would have been one way to see if the supervisors were properly doing their jobs. Had you done so, this disaster may have been averted."

So basically, I am chastised for not being more aggressive in my supervision of my subordinates and receive a written reprimand. I don't like that; I had never had any form of reprimand or discipline in my entire career.

Looking back at everything, trying to be objective, I guess I do deserve it.

After getting my reprimand, I take the rest of the week off. I am emotionally drained. I am also a little disappointed in myself. I considered myself to be a good district manager, even a possible candidate for chief operating officer. But apparently, I have not done my very best and have at least partial blame in this tragedy.

When I return the next week, I find that employee morale is at an all-time low given that two well-liked employees were fired. This time, I insist that the CEO come out, address our district office, and explain the circumstances. He doesn't visit the offices often, so when he does come, it makes a big impact. Fortunately, he agrees to come. He explains to everyone how having those big moving vans out on the road is dangerous and we have to be extra cautious in everything we do. Again, he is a good public speaker, and I think he hit the mark. The employees seem to understand why we did what we did, and slowly morale starts to pick up. Within a few weeks, we seem to be back to normal. Life does move on.

Carla, whom I had left in charge, handled that matter with Fred from the Anderson Company. She told Fred that we believed our driver's version of events. However, since he was such a good customer, we would honor his claim and make reimbursement. Carla knew that she did not really have the authority to do that. But she knew that checking with me during that crisis seemed unnecessary.

She was thinking on her feet and instinctively knew that I would appreciate her taking control like that. It was not an important issue in relation to our accident, but from Fred's perspective, it was very important. So, she handled it and allowed business to continue on during this crisis.

Following the accident, business seems to have slowed down for us across the nation. It isn't a tremendous slow-down, but it is at a time of year when activity tends to pick up. Our competitors use the accident to their advantage, making subtle references to it in their advertising. During one of our managerial videoconferences, we discuss an aggressive counter-advertising campaign. It sounds enticing, to get out there and fight for our name. Then we decide against it; that is just a knee-jerk reaction. We would only accomplish keeping the issue alive. We ignore our competitors. It takes a few months, but the accident becomes old news, and our business comes back and continues to grow.

By the end of the following year, my district has performed admirably. We generated record revenues and had the lowest damage claims of all districts. There were no accidents and there no customer complaints that could not be resolved at the local level. It is great news to report at our end-of-year all-employees' conference. That seems to give morale a boost. Generally, employees do take pride in their work and like to see that there is some benefit from their efforts.

I receive my Annual Performance Appraisal, which is rated as "Superior." I feel really good; I have redeemed myself and think that I might again be on that corporate ladder. Come the end of December, I am a little surprised that I do not get a bonus. When the chief operating officer position opens up several months later, I am not selected. The CEO has an honest conversation with me. He tells me, "When such a tragedy occurs under your watch, it is unlikely that you can avoid any blame or responsibility; real or perceived, fair or not. It would not have been good public relations for the company to give me a promotion so soon after that tragedy. The interests of the company come first. That's how it goes."

I learned a lot about problem solving on the day of the tragic accident—from the small issues of switching days off to customer service to responding to a crisis. There were many things that could have been done differently and that may have changed the course of events. Second-guessing and beating ourselves up over past events is wasteful and counterproductive. Taking an honest look at ourselves, acknowledging mistakes, and believing we can change and improve both ourselves and our way of doing business, will lead to fewer crises and more success.

As for me, I retired from the moving industry. I now give lectures on all that I learned from those few days.

CHAPTER 24

Lesson: What Does It All Mean?
Or, "Is the Whole Greater Than the Sum of the Parts?"

We've explored ideas and concepts that have applied to real-life situations in both business and personal lives. We've taken a look at these ideas from a fictional, yet realistic point of view. We have looked at all sorts of events and theories and schools of thought. I hope the stories have amused you, enlightened you, and given you something to think about. The concepts presented in this book are based on my observations and experiences of a twenty-seven year law enforcement career and are offered for your consideration.

The chapters do not represent one particular theory of management for dealing with the intricacies of business life or human relationships. I do not believe that there is any one theory of management that can address all the problems and challenges that we confront in our average business day. The world of business processes is too complex, too dynamic, and too unpredictable to be able to employ one specific theory. We must recognize that there are limits on what we can control and change. You can provide an environment that promotes and encourages motivation, creativity, and productivity but you cannot motivate people who refuse to be motivated.

While you cannot eliminate all risks and vulnerabilities, you must identify them and minimize them, proactively. You should position yourself to be able to identify and exploit new methods and opportunities. You must call out your SWOT team and conduct your own SWOT analysis to identify your Strengths, Weaknesses, Opportunities and Threats, and be prepared to act. Otherwise, opportunities will pass you by. You may survive, but you will not thrive. If you do not improve your weaknesses and prepare for your threats, you may not even survive.

I especially recognized the value of some of the things we discussed in this book while reading the February 8, 2007, edition of *The Wall Street Journal*. On the front page, the first article I noticed, written by Jeanne Cummings, was entitled "Political Hazard: Candidates Bilked by Their Treasurers." The article discussed that the treasurer stole $94,000 from a candidate's campaign funds. Cummings pointed out, "What happened...isn't uncommon in campaigns because candidates trust friends to handle the money and often don't look too carefully at their work." Does this not sound familiar to some of the managerial lapses we discussed that led to serious problems—turning only to those whom we know and are comfortable with, then relying on that comfort with no internal controls or adequate oversight in place?

Right next to that article was another article entitled "In Home Lending Push, Banks Misjudged Risk," written by Carrick Mollenkamp. The article discussed, "When the U.S. housing market was booming, HSBC Holdings PLC raced to join the party. Sensing opportunity in the bottom end of the mortgage market, the giant British bank bet big on borrowers with sketchy credit records. Such subprime customers have always been risky, but HSBC figured it could control that risk." Now with many of those loans in arrears and borrower fraud becoming evident, the author points out that "HSBC reached a disconcerting conclusion: Its system for screening subprime borrowers and assessing the default risk they posed were flawed." Not only do we see poor risk management in this case, one must wonder if entering into the mortgage market towards the bottom end was nothing more than a knee-jerk reaction that did not undergo adequate analysis. The financial meltdown of 2009 was the culmination of poor risk management, ineffective business processes, and weak internal controls.

Enron, WorldCom, Tyco, Arthur Andersen, Lehman Brothers, AIG and General Motors were high profile debacles. These corporate calamities may have been averted by strong internal controls, stopping and thinking, and someone questioning the integrity and values reflected by corporate and individual actions. Did a two-million-dollar birthday party, partially funded by a corporation, really pass the "smell test"? Maybe somewhere there was an appropriate part for the morality police to play. Was there a business culture that promoted and welcomed individual thought and dissension, or did executives, officers and directors plunge into groupthink? While we must place a certain amount of trust in our leaders, *doverey no proverey*. That is Russian for what President Reagan said to Soviet President Mikhail Gorbachev during the signing of the Intermediate Rand Nuclear Forces Treaty of 1987: trust but verify.

Not all good decisions yield good results. Not all bad decisions yield bad results; sometimes you get lucky. Life is not fair and is not predictable; accept that. Pay attention to your responsibilities and your personnel. Approach your work with a sense of commitment and a dedication to improvement and excellence. Demand and display the highest level of ethics and values. Think long term. Don't shoot from the hip. Don't rush to judgment. Listen to others, especially your subordinates; they have their ear to the ground. Put the interests of the team and the organization first. Trust your instinct. Have confidence in yourself. Yet, recognize your weaknesses and work to improve them. Acknowledge and respect the strengths in others and use them. Give credit when credit is deserved. Treat everyone with respect, compassion, and dignity. These concepts do not form one cohesive theory of management. They are just rational ways to address life's little and big challenges. Most of all, even in the face of great adversity, never lose your sense of humor; it will see you through. Then, watch your people and your organization grow and prosper.

Good luck.